Real Japanese

Learn to speak the same way Japanese kids do!

MARK SMITH

2010

Illustrated by Miho Yasunaga

About the author:

A computer programmer by profession, Mark Smith has spent 12 years in Japan. His main qualification for writing this book is that most of his friends seem to be Japanese 4 year olds. Despite having a black belt in the martial art of Aikido, he is still bullied by these friends, and also by his wife, and two half-Japanese children, both toddlers. His dream is to divide his time between Tokyo and New Zealand, but he doesn't really like flying.

Special thanks to:

My wife Hiroko, who both tolerated and helped me;
my daughters, who inspired me;
my brother Andrew, who encouraged me;
and my parents, for their faith in me.

Contents

Introduction 2

Two years: The first six months 12

Two years: Month seven 19

Two years: Month eight 37

Two years: Month nine 50

Two years: Month ten 68

Two years: Month eleven 81

Two years: Month twelve 98

Three years: Month one 115

Three years: Month two 130

Three years: Month three 145

Three years: Month four 155

Three years: Month five 164

Three years: Month six 174

Final Comments 184

Verb Reference 186

Introduction

Children begin to speak in sentences of more than one word at around two years of age, and by the time they are three years old they have a vocabulary of 300 to 500 words. Of course each child develops at his/her own pace, but most three year old Japanese children can construct fairly complex sentences such as these:

takusan asonda kara tsukareteru	-	I played a lot so I'm tired
uragaeshi ni natchatta yo	-	It has gone inside out!
nottara ii ja nai?	-	Wouldn't it be okay to ride?

They have not simply memorized these sentences: They can use them spontaneously and can make endless variations. If you have studied Japanese before, you may be amazed that children could achieve this level of proficiency in only twelve months of speaking. However it is actually a natural progression resulting from the order in which children pick up their vocabulary and grammar.

Real Japanese illustrates the way Japanese children learn to speak their own language. Every new language point spoken by an actual child is listed here, in a day by day format. This is a very different approach to the way Japanese is generally taught in textbooks and language courses, which introduce grammar using contrived conversations. Every sentence here is real Japanese, as spoken by a Japanese child.

But Real Japanese is not a typical phrase-book. Each entry is listed on the day it was first spoken. Most demonstrate the use of a new verb, a new verb form (such as a different tense), a new adjective or a new grammatical structure. Some are included because they are particularly useful or common, or show how a construct can be used in a different context. However phrases are not included simply to present new vocabulary.

Children can understand more than they are able to speak themselves, but it is only once they start to actually use language points that they master them. This book therefore follows a logical, natural order, even though it may at first appear to be an arbitrary selection of sentences.

A unique approach

Traditional textbooks and language courses use a given dialog or situation to teach particular vocabulary and grammar, starting with simple grammar and advancing to more complex structures. However the vocabulary and grammar are then difficult to remember, and even if you manage to memorize whole sentences from the passage, they are unlikely to be useful in any real situation. For instance, after studying a lesson on "Taking a taxi", it can be a frustrating experience to actually ride in a taxi in Japan and find that nothing from the lesson could be applied.

The idea behind Real Japanese is that like most subjects, a language cannot be taught, it can only be learned. Grammar and vocabulary dictionaries are indispensible for reference. But grammar in particular is best picked up in the same natural way as anything else we learn, and that is by encountering small pieces of new knowledge that build on our previous knowledge, and seeing it applied in a way that makes sense to us.

It is the aim of this book to present the basics of the Japanese language using this radical new method that we hope will allow the reader to communicate effectively in a much shorter time.

Why 2 to 3.5 years?

We found that children learn a lot of vocabulary and grammar between the ages of two and three and a half years old. After that they concentrate more on accumulating vocabulary. The focus of this book is on grammar and useful common vocabulary, so as a result the chapters towards the end are shorter in length.

Where are the particles?

Particles are the words that connect up the verbs, nouns, objects etc in a sentence, like prepositions in English. Some common ones are "*o*", "*ni*", "*de*", "*wa*" and "*ga*". You won't find many particles in the earlier parts of this book, and that is simply because two year olds hardly ever use them.

Children first concentrate on learning vocabulary and the word order of Japanese sentences, and only begin to use particles when they are necessary to get the meaning across. Later, at around three years of age, they start dropping in more and more particles as they attempt longer and more complex sentences.

Textbooks naturally require every sentence to be grammatically correct, so some teachers might object to the particles being left out. But in the informal level of speech used by children it is common to omit most particles, just as it is for Japanese people of any age when they use this level of speech.

The trick to speaking without particles is to avoid pausing between words. If you manage to sound confident, a Japanese friend is less likely to try to "help" you by "correcting" your sentences.

Levels of speech

Students of Japanese are normally taught the neutral or polite level of speech first, which uses the "desu/-masu" verb forms. This is considered the safest approach, and least likely to cause offense. However it is also rarely appropriate for any given real situation. It is usually either too polite or too informal, and tends to make men sound like women!

Real Japanese mostly uses the informal level of speech, which is characterized by the use of "plain" or "-ru" verb forms. Once again, this is because these are genuine sentences and this is how children speak.

Although starting with informal speech is contrary to traditional methods of teaching Japanese, it makes sense for a number of reasons:

> Japanese people actually *think* using informal speech, mostly without particles, and then adjust the speech level and add particles in only when they vocalize a sentence. They use informal speech when they mutter to themselves under their breath. They use it when they get angry or emotional. To some degree we do this in English too, using different language when thinking vs. chatting with a friend vs. talking to our boss vs. making a presentation vs. giving a speech.

> Neutral and formal speech are extensions of informal speech. Once you have the foundation of informal speech, you can add neutral speech and then formal speech. It is more difficult to go the other way, which is why many students struggle to learn to speak slang, even after years of studying neutral and formal Japanese.

> Informal speech tends to be shorter:

> "I'd like some pizza"
> **watashi wa pizza o tabetai desu**   (Neutral)
> **pizza tabetai**   (Informal)

> Men and women do not speak the same in Japanese. They use different levels of politeness, and even many differ-

ent words. However when using informal speech this distinction is not made, and they can usually speak exactly the same way. This makes life easier for students learning informal speech, and also for young children who are not yet even aware different genders exist! On the few occasions when masculine or feminine speech is used, this is noted in the text.

A word of caution

Please be aware that informal speech is not suitable for everyone. In particular it is not appropriate for any kind of formal situation. It is not going to be useful to someone looking for a few phrases to use in a business situation. You shouldn't really use it with anyone older or more senior than yourself, although Japanese people will normally appreciate your efforts to speak their language and be kind enough to let you get away with it. And it will certainly not help you pass Japanese tests at school!

This level of speech is acceptable for written communications, including email and the internet, but only when you want to sound informal.

Of course you can continue to use other methods of study while using this book. You will gain an additional perspective on the Japanese language, and a better basis for how to think in Japanese when you want to really communicate rather than just study grammar.

Grammatical ground rules

Children are very accepting when presented with new knowledge, even when it is incomplete and seems contradictory. They store it all away, and make sense of it later when they have enough information to piece it all together. Adults on the other hand, tend to feel uncomfortable with this. They want to have the rules laid out explicitly as in a textbook. However you will gain a more natural grasp of Japanese if you try to soak up the grammatical rules through examples, as children do. Focus on communicating instead of creating a perfect sentence.

It is often said that children have an advantage over adults because their brains are hard-wired at this age for learning a language. However they also have many other new things to learn at the same time, and have no reference points to help them understand new grammar or vocabulary. When learning from Real Japanese, you also have the advantage of notes that explain new material.

The English translations here are not always word-for-word literal translations, which can often sound stilted even though they might be technically more accurate. Instead, we have tried to capture the meaning of each phrase as accurately as possible in natural English. As a result, you may not be able to match every single word to the corresponding word in the English translation. Just accept the meaning of the translation, and concentrate on the Japanese.

Is this baby talk? Is it slang?

There is almost no slang used in this book, since young children haven't learned to use slang yet. The informal level of speech used may look like slang, since slang terms appear most often in that kind of speech. But the vocabulary here is not slang, and can generally be used in other levels of speech. As such, the sentences here should not become dated over time.

It isn't baby talk either though. Some of the most common recognizable first sounds or words of Japanese babies are:

mee	-	The sound a sheep makes, i.e. "baa"
bappa	-	"*papa*" (Father) or "*happa*" (leaves)

manmaa	-	"*mama*" (Mother) or "*manma*" (baby talk for cooked rice)
baai	-	"*baibai*" (Bye bye)
nannan	-	"*nani*" / "*nan da*" (what?)

Other first words not so easily identified include "*aaa*", "*awawa*" and "*bee*".

Clearly there would be little point in learning to babble like a baby. So we have spared you this stage, and instead begin at the point where a child is able to pronounce the sounds needed for words. They are at the far more interesting point of having already built a small vocabulary of words, and are ready to start making sentences.

This book follows the progress of a single girl, referred to as "A-chan". Although each child picks up different vocabulary depending on their environment, the grammar learned by all children at a particular stage is surprisingly consistent.

Some of the sentences reflect the things that become important to a child at various ages. For example, the topic of going to the toilet appears more often than an adult might discuss such things. But in general we hope you find the vocabulary used here to be useful at any age. You will quickly build a vocabulary relevant to your own situation when you speak with Japanese people yourself, and should be able to slot them into the grammar learned in this book.

Practice makes perfect

Focused repetition is the key to learning anything that involves memorization.

Children practice by repeating new phrases almost compulsively, nearly driving their parents crazy in the process. They add variations, and try out many possible combinations. They might apply a newly-acquired verb tense to every verb they can think of, or add a particular sentence ending to every sentence they speak. Then they suddenly move on to practicing something else.

Life is a game to children. They are constantly playing, no matter what else they might be doing at the time, such as eating, dressing or crossing the road. Consequently, their speech seems to have two modes:

Mostly they are in 'Practice' mode, which is how they talk while playing. Their sentences follow their imaginations, they babble nonsense, they change subject in the middle of a sentence, and importantly, they continually experiment with their language and repeat things over and over. They often use this mode when talking to themselves, and to other children or adults.

The other mode is a kind of 'Communications' mode, where they want someone else to understand what they are saying. So their speech becomes a little slower and clearer. They even use hand gestures if necessary, and of course they treat you like an idiot if you don't understand.

Try to emulate these modes in your own study. You can practice alone by making up silly games, telling a story, or talking to yourself about topics that interest you. It doesn't matter, just keep talking. It is also important to have role models for your language, just as children do, so find opportunities to speak regularly with native speakers. A language cannot be learned just by reading a book, so however you decide to practice, make sure it involves speaking out loud.

Another point to note is that children are not afraid to make mistakes, and sometimes a phrase may become a favorite for weeks on end even though it is not correct. This book also shows many of the mistakes made by A-*chan*, which give an extra insight into her thinking processes.

We encourage you to read the chapters in order, starting from the beginning. Memorize and practice the sentences, adapt them to what you want to say, and use them as often as possible with Japanese people.

Conventions used in this book

Due to space constraints, the entries here are not shown in Japanese characters. While the study of the Japanese writing system is fascinating and useful, the aim of this book is communication. It is vital that your speech be as smooth as possible, which would be difficult for many readers if the Roman characters were not included. Besides, young children learn to speak before beginning to read or write.

The Hepburn style of Romanization is used, with the exception that the long vowels for 'o' (おう) and 'u' (うう) are written as 'ou' and 'uu' instead of 'ō' and 'ū'. This convention is taken from the 'Wāpuro Rōmaji' variation, and more accurately represents the way these long vowels are written in hiragana and katakana. Other long vowels are written as 'aa', 'ii' and 'ee' for consistency.

Pronunciation

It is assumed the reader has access to a good Japanese dictionary, which is bound to include a guide to pronunciation. Readers not already familiar with basic pronunciation are referred to their dictionaries rather than reproducing the details here.

It is also useful to listen carefully to the intonation of a native speaker. Some textbooks try to indicate tonal patterns, but the results tend to be confusing and distracting.

A note about names

You may be wondering why people's names are not used in this book. Sentences without names are not only easier to memorize, they take up less space on the page.

To keep a consistent Japanese accent when reading the sentences, you should pronounce "A-*chan*" as "*ei-chan*", "C-*chan*" as "*shii-chan*", "M-*chan*" as "*emu-chan*" etc. The suffix "-*chan*" is added after the first name of young girls, and "-*kun*" for young boys. When speaking with adults, you should instead use their surname only, and append "-*san*". Do not append a suffix to your own name.

Names of characters such as Mickey Mouse and Cinderella are written in full, since they add to the context of the phrases.

Give it a go!

We hope Real Japanese gives you a unique look at how Japanese people learn their own language, and provides a basis for ongoing study. It is not easy to learn a new language. But remember this: If a two year old child can do it, then so can you!

Two years:
The first six months

During this period children learn to mimic many words and phrases. They are often doing little more than copying sounds and associating meaning with them, so they are only just beginning to have a concept of grammar. They can only create very simple variations of phrases. So it is safe for you to memorize them too, without worrying too much about the details of their construction.

This chapter introduces a lot of initial vocabulary. The first words vary widely per child, but the ones below will give you a good start. Subsequent chapters will only list new language points.

The very first words spoken by A-chan were:

Mama	-	Mummy
Papa	-	Daddy
atchi	-	That way

Then she learned the names for many things, such as:

Parts of the body	*te*	-	hand
	ashi	-	leg / foot
	kuchi	-	mouth
	me	-	eye
	mimi	-	ear
	oshiri	-	bottom
Clothing	*sokkusu*	-	socks
	doresu	-	dress
	buutsu	-	boots
	kutsu	-	shoes
	surippa	-	slippers

Colors	*aka*	-	red
	ao	-	blue[1]
	kiiro	-	yellow
	guriin	-	green
Around the home	*burashi*	-	(hair) brush
	taoru	-	towel
	ofuro	-	bath
	beddo	-	bed
	hooku	-	fork
	supuun	-	spoon
	pasokon	-	computer
	terebi	-	television
	denwa	-	phone
	hon	-	book
Outside	*ki*	-	tree
	happa	-	leaves
	hana	-	flower
Animals	*wanwan*	-	doggy[2]
	neko	-	cat
	osakana	-	fish
	kaeru	-	frog
Transport	*kuruma*	-	car
	densha	-	train
	torakku	-	truck
	shinkansen	-	bullet train
	eki	-	station

A-chan also learned the names of friends, relatives and toys, and various foods and vegetables.

---

[1] 'ao' can also mean green-blue, like the green in traffic lights.
[2] 'wanwan' is a baby word, like 'bow-wow' in English.

Then she added these phrases and adjectives:

gomen nasai	-	I'm sorry
hai	-	Yes
douzo	-	Go ahead
hai douzo	-	Okay, go ahead
[name] *douzo*	-	Go ahead, [name]
yada!	-	No![3]
iya desu!	-	No![4]
tadaima	-	I'm home
are?	-	Eh? / What? (Surprised)
arigatou	-	Thanks
suimasen	-	Excuse me / Thank you[5]
konnichi wa	-	Hello
ohayou	-	Good morning
dekita (yo)	-	I did it[6]
[name] *ita yo*	-	[name] was there
dete kita yo	-	It came out
detenai yo	-	It hasn't come out
owatchatta	-	It's all finished[7]
mite / mite mite	-	Look / Look look
akete kudasai	-	Please open it
Papa, keshite kudasai	-	Daddy, turn it off please
kashite (kudasai)	-	Lend it to me (please) / Can I have it?
chotto matte te (kudasai)	-	(Please) wait a minute[8]
terebi tsukete kudasai	-	Please turn the television on

---

[3] Properly spelt '*iya da*', but the '*i*' is not pronounced.
[4] Literally 'It is disagreeable'.
[5] '*suimasen*' is a contraction of '*sumimasen*' (Excuse me / Thank you).
[6] Literally 'I could do it'.
[7] The '-chatta' form means to have done something by mistake, or to have done it completely.
[8] With '*te*' this phrase literally means 'Please be *waiting* a little', but it is also common without it.

Otousan itte	-	Daddy, you go[9]
chuu shite	-	Kiss me[10]
chuu shita	-	We kissed
denwa kudasai	-	Please phone
denwa shiyou	-	Let's phone
ocha nomu	-	I'll drink tea[11]
shitenai (yo)	-	I haven't done it
mou ikkai mite ii?	-	Can I watch it again?
mou ikkai yaru?	-	Will we do it again? / Shall we do it again?
baburu yatte ii?	-	Can I do bubbles?
mada tabeteru	-	I'm still eating
nani shiteru no?	-	What are you doing?
kore	-	This
kore wa?	-	How about this?
nan da kore? / kore nani? / nani kore?	-	What's this?
Anpanman da yo kore!	-	This is Anpanman![12]
onaji	-	The same
onaji da ne (kore)	-	(This is) the same, isn't it
A-chan no!	-	It's A-chan's![13]
daijoubu?	-	Are you okay? / Are you alright?
daijoubu	-	I'm okay / I'm alright
itai no	-	It hurts
itakatta	-	It hurt (past tense)
kusuguttai	-	It tickles

---

[9] '*Otousan*' is more like 'Father', but we will use 'Daddy' for both '*Otousan*' and '*Papa*'.
[10] '*chuu*' is used mainly by children and women.
[11] '*ocha*' often refers to green tea, but it can also mean other kinds of tea like '*mugicha*' (barley tea) and '*houjicha*' (roasted green tea). Western tea is always called '*koucha*'.
[12] '*kore*' at the end makes it literally 'It's Anpanman, *this is!*'
[13] '*no*' here shows possession or ownership.

atsui	-	It's hot
atsukunai	-	It's not hot
kore to kore to...	-	This and this and...
[object] *to* [object] *to...*	-	[Object] and [object] and...
atchi ikou	-	Let's go that way
iku yo	-	I'm going
mou chotto yaru yo	-	I'll do it a bit more
mou ikkai yaru no	-	I'll do it once more
jouzu da ne	-	You're good at it, aren't you
[name] *wa?*	-	What about [name]?
Okaasan nani shiteru?	-	What's Mummy doing?[14]
akachan naiteru yo	-	The baby is crying
akachan naichatta nee	-	The baby cried, didn't she?
oshikko morechatta	-	My wee leaked
ribon tsuiteru	-	It has a ribbon attached
omoi	-	It's heavy
tsumetai	-	It's cold (to the touch)
denki iranai	-	I don't need (want) the lights
guru guru mawasu	-	You turn it round and round
guru guru mawashite	-	Turn it round and round
ochichatta	-	It fell down
minna ni aru yo	-	There's some for everyone
aru yo	-	There is one / There are some
dakko	-	Hold / carry / hug
ombu	-	Piggy-back ride
kataguruma	-	Shoulder ride

---

[14] '*Okaasan*' is more like 'Mother', but we will use 'Mummy' for both '*Okaasan*' and '*Mama*'.

Two years: The first six months

"*douzo*" - Have some!

Notes

- Most Japanese words do not have plurals. So for example, '*te*' can mean either one hand or both hands.

- '*da*' means 'is/am/are' etc, and is used in almost the same way as '*desu*' in the neutral speech level.

- You can add '*yo*' to the end of any sentence to add emphasis, almost like an exclamation mark in English.

- Adding '*no*' at the end of a phrase turns a statement into an explanation, or softens a question. So '*nani shiteru no?*' means 'What *is it* you're doing?', and '*itai no*' means 'It's *that* it hurts' or '*Since* it hurts'.

- Personal pronouns are often only implied. So depending on the context, '*chuu shita*' could mean 'I kissed you', 'You kissed me', 'He kissed her', or 'They kissed' etc.

- '*nee*' is a longer version of '*ne*', with the same meaning. Both solicit a response when said as a question, like '*ne?*' and '*nee?*'.

> You can use your own name to mean "me" or "I". So for example, when A-chan says '*A-chan no!*, she means "It's mine!". This sounds childish if overused, and often it is better to omit your name altogether if the meaning is clear from the context. Later you will see A-chan begins to use '*watashi*', which is safe for both males and females. Children shouldn't use '*-chan*' or '*-kun*' after their own names, but at this age they don't know that.

Two years: Month seven

Day 1

dekinai	-	I can't do it
tsukutteru	-	I'm making it
kore M-chan ga kureta	-	M-chan gave me this
kore kawaii	-	This is cute
koko yaru	-	I'll do it here[1]
kore pinku da yo!	-	This is pink!
kore nani kore?	-	This, what is this?
atta!	-	Here it is! / I found it![2]
kore douzo	-	Here, take this
Papa machigaeta	-	Daddy did it wrong
yonde kuru	-	I will go and call her[3]
yonde kita	-	I went and called her
kono shitagi kawaii nee	-	This underwear is so cute
mata ashita	-	See you again tomorrow[4]

Day 2

Okaasan, A-chan naichatta	-	Mummy, A-chan cried
Okaasan okotchatta	-	Mummy got angry
tsugi wa...	-	Next...
kirei!	-	It's pretty![5]
ii yo	-	That's okay / Okay (Giving permission)
oite kudasai	-	Please put it there / Please leave it
oishii	-	It's yummy / It's tasty / It tastes good
tanoshikatta	-	It was fun
ookii	-	It's big

---

[1] '*koko de yaru*' would be better.
[2] Literally 'It was'.
[3] A-chan learned '*yonde*' meaning 'call' before '*yonde*' meaning 'read'.
[4] Literally just 'Again tomorrow'.
[5] As noted before, the subject is omitted so this could also mean "She is pretty", "They are pretty" etc, depending on the context.

chiisai	-	It's small
mimi itakatta	-	My ears hurt (past tense) / It hurt my ears
iranai	-	I don't want it / I don't need it
mitai kore	-	I want to see this
hantai wa?	-	What about the other (opposite) one?
chokichoki shiteru	-	I'm cutting (with scissors)[6]
nenne suru	-	I will have a sleep[7]
atode miru	-	I will watch it later
ochita	-	It fell down
dore ga ii no?	-	Which one do you want?
isu motte kudasai	-	Please bring a chair
kou yatte	-	Do it like this
Papa yatte	-	Daddy, you do it
ame futte kita	-	It has started raining
ame futteru yo	-	It is raining
A-chan no kasa wa?	-	What about A-chan's umbrella? / Where is A-chan's umbrella?
sou sou	-	Yes, that's it
daiji / daiji da yo	-	It's precious
isshoni ikou	-	Let's go together
matteru yo	-	I'm waiting

Common mistakes

densha yaru	-	We will take the train[8]
densha yatta	-	We took the train[9]

---

[6] '*chokichoki*' is a children's word.
[7] '*nenne*' is a children's word, like 'bed-time' or 'beddy-byes'.
[8] Should be '*densha de iku*'. However '*densha yaru*' could be used to mean 'We will play trains'.
[9] Should be '*densha de itta*'.

Day 3

dakko suru	-	I will carry you
dakko suru?	-	Will you carry me?
toreru	-	I can get it
mata kuru kara ne	-	We'll come here again though, won't we[10]
minna ni aru ka naa?	-	I wonder whether there's some for everyone?
minna ni baibai shiyou	-	Let's say bye bye to everyone
minna ni baibai shiteta	-	I was saying bye bye to everyone[11]
A-chan oshiri yaru yo	-	We will change A-chan's nappy[12]
nande ka naa?	-	I wonder why?
Otousan yatta, kore?	-	Daddy did you do this?
douzo oite kite	-	Please go and put it there
tsuite kara	-	After we arrive[13]
kouen iku?	-	Will we go to the park? / Shall we go to the park?[14]
jinja ikou	-	Let's go to the shrine
mou ii kai? mou ii yo!	-	Are you ready? I'm ready![15]
shiroi gohan iranai	-	I don't want white rice[16]
soto de jampu shite	-	Jump outside[17]
mukou de yaru	-	I'll do it over there
Otousan kakkou ii	-	Daddy is cool[18]

---

[10] '*kara*' means 'because', so this is literally 'Because we will come again'.
[11] '*shiteta*' means 'was doing'.
[12] Literally 'A-chan will do her bottom'.
[13] '*kara*' after the '-te' verb form means '*after*'.
[14] '*iku?*' means 'Will we go?', but here it is used in place of '*ikou?*' (Shall we go?).
[15] These are set phrases for playing hide and seek.
[16] An adjective with a noun for the first time: '*shiroi gohan*' meaning 'white rice'.
[17] '*de*' means 'at', 'in' or 'by'.
[18] A-chan probably thinks of the expression '*kakkou ii*' as a single word.

Day 4

oshikko ga dete kichatta	-	My wee has come out
tabete kita	-	I ate there / I've already eaten[19]
mienai	-	I can't see it
dekimashita	-	I could do it / I did it[20]
irasshaimase!	-	Welcome! (into a shop)
misetai	-	I want to show it to you
Inai Inai Baa hajimatta	-	Inai Inai Baa has started[21]

Common mistakes

Inai Inai Baa hajimatte kichatta	-	Inai Inai Baa has started[22]

Day 5

okita	-	She is up / She got up
omutsu kaenai	-	I won't change my nappy
omutsu kaeteru	-	I am changing my nappy
kowashichatta yo	-	I've broken it / I've gone and broken it
onigiri setto tabete kita yo	-	I went there and ate the rice-balls set meal

Common mistakes

asobete kudasai	-	Please play[23]

Day 6

nan deshou?	-	What's that?[24]
gohan ga ii no	-	I want rice

---

[19] Literally 'I ate it and came back'.
[20] The polite '*-mashita*' form, which A-chan pronounces very deliberately: '*deki-ma-shi-ta*'.
[21] Inai Inai Baa is a popular NHK television program for young children.
[22] '*hajimatte kichatta*' doesn't make sense.
[23] The correct '*-te*' form of asobu (to play) is '*asonde*'.
[24] '*deshou*' means 'probably', so literally 'What is this probably?'. This softens the question and makes it sound less like a demand.

Two years: Month seven

isshoni yaru	-	We'll do it together
A-chan yaru	-	A-chan will do it
motto kudasai	-	More please
tabete kita kara daijoubu	-	I ate before coming so I'm okay[25]

Common mistakes

kore dare?	-	Who is this?[26]

Day 7

nee nee	-	Hey[27]
tsukatte ii?	-	Can I use it?
mite, dekiagari!	-	Look, all done!
ja, boku wa suru	-	Then, I'll do it[28]
daijoubu da nee	-	It's all okay

Day 8

motte ii no?	-	Is it okay if I hold it?
oite te	-	Leave it
kaiteru	-	I'm drawing / I'm writing
tatte	-	Stand up
epuron wasureta no	-	We forgot my apron
hairu?	-	Will we go in?
herikoputaa datte	-	He says it's a helicopter
A-chan mo iku n datte	-	She says A-chan will go too[29]
omoshiroi nee	-	It's so interesting
tomete	-	Stop (here)
zannen da na	-	What a shame / What a pity[30]
kawaisou da na	-	You poor thing

---

[25] Literally 'I ate and came here so I'm okay'.
[26] '*kore*' should only be used for objects, not people.
[27] '*nee*' used like this is feminine speech.
[28] Girls shouldn't really use '*boku*'.
[29] '*mo*' means 'also' or 'too'.
[30] '*na*' is form of '*ne*' used more by males.

Common mistakes

chigau da yo	-	That's wrong / You're wrong[31]
atarashii da yo	-	It's new[32]

Day 9

saki ni kore	-	This first
saki ni douzo	-	You go first
kore, hana ga ookii no	-	This has big flowers
neko-chan inai?	-	Aren't there any pussy cats?[33]
tsunaide kudasai	-	Please connect them
Mama ga ita yo	-	There's Mummy[34]
koko itai	-	It hurts here
oshiri itai	-	My bottom hurts

Day 10

ame futte kuru yo	-	It's going to rain
datte...	-	Well because...
guru guru mawasu?	-	Will you turn it round and round?
M-chan gacha gacha suki	-	M-chan likes gacha gacha toys[35]
gacha gacha miitsuketa	-	I found the gacha gacha toy[36]
boku wa mite kuru kara	-	I'll just go and see[37]
A-chan dekiru kara	-	Because A-chan can do it (herself)
arigatou! ureshii naa	-	Thanks! I'm so glad
kore nani? nan deshou?	-	What's this? What could it be?
wakannai	-	I don't know / I don't understand
iru	-	I want it / I need it

---

[31] Should be either '*chigau n da yo*' or '*chigau yo*', although some people do actually say '*chigau da yo*'.
[32] Should be either '*atarashii n da yo*' or '*atarashii yo*'.
[33] Note this is a negative question.
[34] Literally 'Mummy was there'.
[35] '*gacha gacha*' are capsule toys from vending machines.
[36] It is childish speech to stretch out '*mitsuketa*' to '*miitsuketa*'.
[37] Literally 'I'll go and see, so...'.

Day 11

Okaasan to Otousan to A-chan katte kita	-	Mummy and Daddy and A-chan went and bought it
boku wa puchi puchi shiteru	-	I'm popping the bubble-wrap[38]
kowai	-	I'm scared
kowakunai	-	I'm not scared
terebi keshite	-	Turn the television off
haiteru	-	I'm wearing (trousers or a skirt)
gomen nee	-	I'm sorry / Excuse me

Day 12

suika tabeteru kara chotto matte kudasai ne	-	I'm eating watermelon so please wait a minute
dashichatta kara daijoubu	-	I spat it all out so it's okay
kotchi ka na	-	Perhaps it's this way (over here)
ippai aru kara...	-	There are lots, so...
A-chan omutsu kaeteru	-	A-chan is changing her nappy
nani tabeteru no?	-	What is it you're eating?
mada aru kara daijoubu	-	There is still some left, so it's okay
Mama tomodachi to asobu	-	Mummy will go out with her friends[39]
kaado kashite	-	Give me the card
NanDeemo neko-chan inai nee	-	There aren't any pussy cats at Nan-Deemo, are there?[40]

---

[38] *'puchi puchi'* means bubble wrap. Other terms for popping it are *'puchi puchi tsubishi'* (bubble wrap popping) or *'puchi puchi o tsubusu'* (to pop bubble wrap), although *'puchi puchi suru'* is commonly used.

[39] *'asobu'* literally means 'to play' or 'to have fun'.

[40] NanDeemo is the name of A-chan's local community centre.

ocha nomu kara chotto matte te ne	-	I'll drink my tea so please wait a minute
onara shichatta, gomen nasai	-	I broke wind, excuse me
Mama chokichoki shiteru kara chotto matte kudasai	-	Mummy is cutting with scissors so please wait a minute
chokichoki shite ii?	-	Can I cut with scissors?

Common mistakes

daijoubu kara	-	It's okay, so...[41]

Notes

> A-chan hears adults speaking in longer sentences, so she tries too, joining phrases using '*kara*' ('because' or 'so'). When she adds more than one '*kara*' at a time, the results can be as awkward as they would be in English. For example '*asobu kara chotto baibai suru kara mata kuru yo*' (I'm going to play, so I'll say bye-bye, so we will come again). She even appends '*kara*' to phrases just for practise, and then follows it with baby talk.

> She also makes sentences longer by using '*-chatta*' (to do by mistake) and '*-te kuru*' (to go and do something). But she often overuses these or uses them inappropriately. She even puts them together, for example '*tabete kichatta*', when she really just meant '*tabete kita*' (we went and ate) or '*tabeta*' (we ate).

Day 13

kasa naosu yo	-	We'll fix the umbrella
mada tsukatteru	-	I'm still using it
tabetai naa	-	I'd like to eat it / I want to eat it
torenai	-	I can't get it / I can't reach it

---

[41] Should be '*daijoubu dakara*'.

kore ga ii	-	I want this (one)

Notes

> A-chan says *'yaru'* (do) and *'yaranai'* (don't do) when she doesn't know the proper verb. For example with *'shawaa'* (shower), *'hikouki'* (plane), and *'zubon'* (trousers).

Day 14

sei no...	-	Ready and... / Ready steady...
ashita yaru	-	I'll do it tomorrow
konai	-	They won't come
taisou yaru	-	I'll do exercises
keshita	-	I turned it off
keshitenai yo	-	I haven't turned it off
kore tabete ii?	-	Can I eat this?
iku ka?	-	Will we go?[42]
ikou	-	Let's go
inai	-	He's not there
inakatta	-	He wasn't there[43]

Common mistakes

tsunaide kuru?	-	Would you connect them for me?[44]

Day 15

Okaasan to nenne suru	-	I'll sleep with Mummy
T-shatsu kiru yo	-	I'll wear a T-shirt
Otousan saki yaru?	-	Will Daddy do it first?
hazukashii	-	I'm embarrassed / How embarrassing
dakko shite kudasai	-	Please carry me

---

[42] *'ka'* used like this is very informal.
[43] *'-nakatta'* is the past negative of a verb.
[44] Should be *'tsunaide kureru?'*.

wakaranai	-	I don't know / I don't understand
shiranai	-	I don't know
motto yatte kudasai	-	Do it more please
hamigaki shinai	-	I won't brush my teeth[45]
Papa hamigaki shiteru yo	-	Daddy is brushing his teeth
ao da yo	-	It's blue / It's green[46]
iretenai kara	-	Because I haven't put it in
mada tsukatteru no	-	But I'm still using it / Because I'm still using it
mada tsukatteru kara	-	Because I'm still using it
ippai aru	-	There are lots
kore yatte ii?	-	Can I do this?
chigau ja nai	-	That's wrong isn't it[47]

Day 16

tonde itchatta	-	It flew away
kaadigan kinai	-	I won't wear my cardigan[48]
NanDeemo A-chan ga iru	-	A-chan will be at NanDeemo
isshoni iku no	-	We'll go together
yamete kudasai	-	Please stop it
abunai desu yo	-	It's dangerous / Look out
ginza tsuita	-	We have arrived at Ginza[49]
Oniisan sugoi ne	-	That man is amazing
bikkuri shichatta ne	-	We were so surprised, weren't we[50]
nani haitteru?	-	What is inside?

---

[45] A-chan incorrectly pronounces '*hamigaki*' (brushing teeth) as '*hagi-maki*'.
[46] This is commonly heard at traffic lights.
[47] '*ja nai*' here means 'isn't it', and can be shortened to '*jan*'. Don't confuse it with '*ja nai [desu]*' meaning 'not'.
[48] '*kaadigan*' is written with '*de*' and a small '*i*': 'カーディガン'.
[49] The particle '*ni*' is implied.
[50] '*-shichatta*' is not really necessary here. It would be better to say '*bikkuri shita ne*'.

Day 17

chigau chigau	-	That's wrong, that's wrong / No, no
bicho bicho	-	It's dripping wet[51]
bicho bicho natta	-	It's (become) dripping wet[52]
yarou	-	Let's do it
burokku yarou ka?	-	Shall we play blocks?
kore chigau	-	This is wrong
kowai hito	-	A scary person / He's a scary person[53]

Day 18

Mama hagu shita	-	I hugged Mummy
oshikko shita	-	I did wees
unchi detenai	-	I haven't done poos
gochisou sama	-	Thank you for the meal (Said when finished eating)
dore miyou ka?	-	Which one shall we watch?
miyou ka naa?	-	Maybe we'll watch it?

Day 19

owatchatta yo	-	It's all finished
oshimai	-	The End / All done
oshimai desu yo	-	It's the end
mieta yo	-	I could see it
Cinderella miru?	-	Will you watch Cinderella?
eto...	-	Um...
nonda		I drank it
nonjatta	-	I drank it / I drank it all[54]

---

[51] Or '*bisho bisho*'.
[52] The particle '*ni*' is implied.
[53] A-chan always pronounces '*hito*' as '*shito*', as it is commonly heard in speech.
[54] Some verbs use '*-jatta*' instead of '*-chatta*'.

Otousan dore ga ii?	-	Daddy, which one do you want?[55]
A-chan kore ga ii	-	A-chan wants this one
pinku ga ii	-	I want the pink one
wakatta	-	I understand / I understood
kore to kore to onaji da ne	-	This is the same as this / They're the same
hajimaru yo	-	It's going to start / It's about to start
hajimatta	-	It has started
Panda-kun obake	-	Panda is a ghost[56]
ocha nomu?	-	Will you drink tea? / Would you like tea?

Day 20

A-chan kore	-	A-chan wants this
A-chan kore suki	-	A-chan likes this one
kyou are suru?	-	Will we do that today?
aru?	-	Are there any?
aru	-	There are some
Otousan, tetsudatte kudasai	-	Daddy, please help me
epuron tsukete kudasai	-	Please put my apron on

Day 21

kakkou ii	-	It looks cool
S-chan soujiki shiteru	-	S-chan is vacuuming
dakara...	-	So...
moshi moshi	-	Hello? (On the phone)
un	-	Yeah
suki ja nai	-	I don't like it
waratta	-	He laughed
okaimono ikou	-	Let's go shopping[57]

---

[55] '*dore*' is used when there are more than two choices.
[56] Note that even '*desu*' or '*da*' can be omitted in very casual speech.
[57] Shopping is normally called just '*kaimono*', but '*okaimono*' tends to be used with children.

yoisho!	-	Heave ho![58]
dotchi ga ii?	-	Which one do you want?[59]

Day 22

dekinakatta	-	I couldn't do it
okinasai!	-	Get up![60]
tsukau yo	-	I'll use it / I'm going to use it
kore Ernie no dakara	-	Because this is Ernie's[61]
kowaretenai	-	It's not broken
A-chan mo pinku	-	A-chan will have pink too
chigau no, kotchi	-	That's wrong, it's this way
kawaisou da ne	-	You poor thing[62]
oshite	-	Push it
kore dou yatte yaru?	-	How do I do this?[63]
Okaasan kaette kuru kara	-	Mummy will come home, (so...)
tori-san da yo!	-	Birds![64]
osoto, tori-san da yo	-	There are birds outside[65]
mada aru yo	-	There are still some left
sutechatta no	-	I threw it away[66]
mou ikkai yaranai	-	I won't do it again
A-chan aruiteru yo	-	A-chan is walking

---

[58] Shows effort or strain.
[59] '*dotchi*' is used when there are two choices. It can also be pronounced '*dochi*'.
[60] '*-nasai*' indicates a command.
[61] '*dakara*' is often used like this at the end of a sentence, literally meaning "so...".
[62] A small variation on the same phrase that previously ended with '*na*'.
[63] '*dou yatte*' means 'how'. Although '*yatte*' seems redundant, it is commonly repeated like this.
[64] In childish speech '*-san*' is added to many (but not all) animal names. '*o*' is sometimes also prefixed, as in '*ouma-san*' (horse).
[65] Literally 'Outside, birds!'. A more proper sentence would be '*soto ni tori-san ga iru*'.
[66] '*no*' used here shows this is an explanation.

poppo pan tabechau no	-	The pigeons eat up the bread[67]
mou kichatta	-	I'm already wearing it / I already put it on
ocha iru no yo	-	I want some tea[68]
kotchi kara hairu	-	We go in from here[69]
daare?	-	Who is it?[70]

Common mistakes

kore tsuiteru yo	-	I'm putting this on[71]
A-chan jibun dekiru	-	A-chan can do it herself[72]

Notes

➤ A-chan is now almost joining sentences, by running phrases together. For example:

dekiru yo. Otousan yatta?	-	I can do it. Has Daddy done it?
tsuitenai. mada	-	We're not there. Yet.

Day 23

Otousan shawaa hairu?	-	Will Daddy have a shower?
haitte	-	Get in / Go in
kami arau?	-	Will we wash my hair?
daijoubu yo	-	It's okay[73]
machigaechatta yo	-	We did it all wrong
doushita?	-	What happened?

---

[67] '*poppo*' is a children's word for 'pigeon'.
[68] '*no yo*' is feminine speech.
[69] '*kara*' here means 'from'.
[70] '*dare*' stretched to '*daare*' is childish speech for emphasis, like 'Who-oo's this?'.
[71] Should be '*kore tsuketeru yo*'.
[72] Should be '*A-chan jibun de dekiru*'.
[73] In feminine speech '*yo*' can be used without '*da*'.

kirei natta	-	They're clean now[74]
akechatta	-	I opened it
hai	-	No[75]

Day 24

sandaru itai	-	His sandal hurts
nanika itai	-	Something hurts

Day 25

oite kichatta	-	I left it there
kushami shita	-	I sneezed

Notes

> A-chan still overuses '*-chatta*', often using it for no reason. For example, when she just means '*kushami shita*' (I sneezed), she also says '*kushami shichatta*' and '*kushami yatchatta*'. These would mean the sneeze was unintentional, as in 'I've gone and sneezed'.

Day 26

kakurembo	-	Hide and seek
jikan da yo!	-	It's time!
chigau ja nai no?	-	Isn't that wrong?
A-chan konnichi wa shita	-	A-chan said hello[76]

Day 27

A-chan chiisai	-	A-chan is small

---

[74] Technically this is missing '*ni*', but in this case the particle can be omitted since it is often shortened to just '*n*' which then merges into '*natta*'.

[75] '*hai*' means '*no*' when in answer to a negative question, for example '*nenne shinai no?*' (Won't you sleep?)

[76] Just like 'to say hello' in English, it's not really correct to use '*konnichi wa*' as a verb, but people do say it.

Otousan ookii	-	Daddy is big
Papa samukatta?	-	Daddy, were you cold? / Daddy, was it cold?
atsui nee	-	It's hot isn't it
atsui no	-	It's hot
A-chan to Papa	-	A-chan and Daddy
hayai	-	It's fast
oritai	-	I want to get down[77]
ii naa!	-	How nice! / I envy you![78]
pinku ga ii naa	-	I want the pink one / The pink one would be nice
mitai naa	-	I want to see it / It would be nice to see it
A-chan daisuki!	-	A-chan loves it![79]

Common mistakes

chiisai da yo	-	It's small[80]

Day 28

Baaba, Jiiji iru?	-	Will Grandma (and) Grandpa be there?[81]
Baaba, Jiiji, itte kuru yo!	-	We're going to see Grandma and Grandpa![82]
mada!	-	Not yet![83]

---

[77] From '*oriru*', which means to get down from something (like a chair), or off something (like a bus or train).
[78] '*naa*' often expresses a more wishful sense than '*nee*', as in 'Wouldn't that be nice?'.
[79] When terms like '*daisuki*' are not followed by '*desu*', they become more informal and more of an exclamation. For example '*daisuki*' ('I love it!') and '*kirei*' ('It's pretty!').
[80] A-chan sometimes uses '*da yo*' after adjectives that end in an '*i*'. For example '*chiisai da yo*' should be just '*chiisai yo*'.
[81] '*Baaba*' and '*Jiiji*' are children's words taken from '*Obaachan*' or '*Obaasan*' (grandma), and '*Ojiichan*' or '*Ojiisan*' (grandpa).
[82] A-chan often omits '*to*' when listing people or objects.
[83] '*mada*' without '*desu*' here is very informal.

oekaki shiteru no	-	I'm drawing pictures / Since I'm drawing pictures[84]
ohana ga nai	-	There are no flowers

Common mistakes

A-chan mo suteki no, kore	-	A-chan's is lovely too, this one[85]

Day 29

ato wa...	-	After that...
daijoubu desu	-	It's okay[86]
chouchou tonderu!	-	The butterfly is flying! / There's a butterfly!
oide!	-	Come here![87]

Notes

➢ A-chan only uses 'desu' in phrases she has heard and memorized.

Day 30

hantai ja nai?	-	Isn't it backwards / Isn't it the wrong way round?[88]
sugoi ame futteru nee	-	It's raining heavily isn't it[89]
wanchan ja nai?	-	Isn't it a doggy?[90]
mazui!	-	Yuck!
mazui jan!	-	Isn't it yucky![91]

---

[84] '*no*' often means '*since*' or '*because*' in an explanation. But it is not only used in replies, and can be used in an unsolicited explanation.
[85] A-chan attempts sentences that are still beyond her. This one should be something like '*A-chan no mo suteki da ne, kore wa*'.
[86] '*daijoubu*' is a very common word, so there are endless variations of usage. '*daijoubu desu*' is the neutral politeness level of speech.
[87] '*oide*' (come) is a command, often used with children.
[88] '*hantai*' means 'opposite'.
[89] '*sugoi*' literally means 'amazing'.
[90] '*wanchan*' is a children's word for 'dog'.
[91] '*jan*' is a contraction of '*ja nai*', but is not used as a question.

oishii jan!	- Isn't it tasty!
A-chan bikkuri shita nee	- A-chan was very surprised wasn't she
tabete ii yo	- You can eat it / You may eat it

Notes

> ➤ A-chan overuses '*ja nai*' and '*jan*', often appending them to make phrases longer.

Day 31

A-chan to Okaasan to Otousan to...	- A-chan and Mummy and Daddy and...
mite mite, sugoi!	- Look look, wow!
hairanai yo	- It doesn't go in there / It won't go in
oyatsu taberu	- I will eat snacks / I will have a snack
kore sentaku shita?	- Did you wash this (in the washing)?

Two years: Month eight

Day 1

atode ne	-	See you later[1]
koborechau	-	It will get spilt[2]
ita	-	She was there
kaette kita	-	She came back
suwatte ii yo	-	You can sit down
yaru	-	I'll do it

Day 2

gotsun shita	-	We banged into each other / We bumped (heads etc)
doite kudasai	-	Please move (out of the way)
kore kitai	-	I want to wear this
sumimasen...	-	Excuse me...

Day 3

yooguruto kudasai	-	Please give me (some) yogurt[3]
ii no?	-	Is it okay?
kureru no?	-	Can I have it? / Are you giving it to me?
Papa no tokei	-	It's Daddy's watch

Common mistakes

itakattenai	-	It didn't hurt[4]

---

[1] Literally 'Later, okay?'.
[2] '-*chau*' is the present/future tense of '-*chatta*', so '*koborechau*' means to 'accidentally spill'.
[3] '*yooguruto*' (ヨーグルト) is sometimes spelt '*youguruto*' (ヨウグルト).
[4] This was in response to '*itakatta?*' (Does it hurt?). It should be '*ita-kunakatta*' (It didn't hurt).

Day 4

Cinderella miyou nee	-	Let's watch Cinderella[5]
Cinderella mienai	-	I can't see Cinderella
ouma-san mienakatta yo	-	I couldn't see the horse
teeburu ni oite kudasai	-	Please put it on the table

Common mistakes

kigaeru dore ga ii?	-	Which one shall I change into?[6]

Day 5

pinku no atarashii	-	The pink one is new
A-chan ushiro iru yo	-	A-chan is behind you[7]
ii yo, mou kaette kudasai	-	It's okay, please go home now
ita nee	-	He was there, wasn't he
sugoi!	-	Wow!
kore sugoi ne	-	This is amazing, isn't it
Papa hana ga deteru?	-	Is Daddy's nose running?[8]
A-chan mada yaru no!	-	A-chan will keep doing it![9]
minna ni kite kara ne	-	After everyone gets theirs[10]
genki natta	-	I feel better now[11]

---

[5] In this book we use English spelling for names, but they should still be pronounced as Japanese, for example '*Shinderera*' (Cinderella).
[6] This would be correct as two sentences: '*kigaeru. dore ga ii?*' (I will change clothes. Which one?). But A-chan wanted to say '*dore ni kigaeyou ka?*' (Which one shall I change into?).
[7] The particle '*ni*' is implied.
[8] She could have omitted '*ga*' here, but instead learned the phrase as '*hana ga deteru*' (Your nose is running).
[9] Literally 'A-chan will still do it!'.
[10] This was while waiting to start eating at a restaurant.
[11] Literally 'I have become vigorous / energetic'. The particle '*ni*' is implied.

Common mistakes

A-chan aru yo	-	A-chan is here[12]

Day 6

Mickey tabechatta no?	-	Did Mickey Mouse eat it?
mae	-	In front
shuppatsu!	-	Off we go!
nenne shichatta nee	-	He went off to sleep
Okaasan itte konai, nenne shiteru	-	Mummy won't go, she's asleep
futari nenne shiteru	-	They are both sleeping[13]
kore motte te	-	Hold this
nenne shitenai	-	She's not asleep / She hasn't slept

Common mistakes

ouma-san notte	-	Put the horse on[14]

Day 7

osouji	-	Cleaning[15]
mou ikko	-	One more
Papa, koko ni ite kudasai	-	Daddy, please stay here[16]
tomatchatta	-	It stopped
minna yatteru	-	Everyone is doing it
tomodachi, koko desu yo	-	My friends, over here
A-chan namechatta	-	A-chan licked it

---

[12] Should use '*iru*' (is/are) for people, not '*aru*' (is/are for objects).
[13] '*futari*' means two people.
[14] Should be '*ouma-san nosete*' (Put the horse on), since '*ouma-san notte*' would mean 'Ride the horse'.
[15] The '*o*' in '*osouji*' is honorific, and can sound childish in casual speech.
[16] '*koko ni ite kudasai*' literally means 'Please be here'.

Common mistakes

ookii yatta	-	I did it big[17]

Day 8

shitteru?	-	Do you know?
kore shitteru?	-	Do you know this?
mada nenne suru?	-	Will you still sleep? / Are you going to sleep more?
Otousan no obentou?	-	Is it Daddy's packed lunch?
hoikuen itte kuru	-	I'm off to nursery school[18]

Day 9

kore katte kita	-	I went and bought this
omutsu kaete asobou	-	Let's change my nappy and play[19]
ippai aru yo	-	There are lots
sugu kuru kara nee	-	I'll come soon / I'll be back soon[20]

Day 10

basu noru	-	We will take the bus[21]
kitenai	-	She hasn't come
nonde kudasai	-	Please drink it
mou ikko wa?	-	What about the other one?
hippatte	-	Pull it

Day 11

kore mo	-	This too / This one too
kore mo kudasai	-	Please give me this too / I'd like this too please

---

[17] Said on playground swings, she meant '*takaku yatta*' (I went high).
[18] '*itte kuru*' makes this literally 'I will go and come (back)'.
[19] Here two phrases are joined using the '*-te*' verb form.
[20] The trailing '*kara*' here means 'so...', implying '... so please wait', or '... so don't worry' etc.
[21] The particle '*ni*' is implied.

Otousan, okite	-	Daddy, get up
oneesan	-	The young lady[22]

Common mistakes

atarashii no doresu	-	It's a new dress / The new dress[23]

Day 12

Otousan, okiyou	-	Daddy, let's get up[24]
Okaasan okotteru	-	Mummy is angry
okotchau	-	She will get angry
Otousan kore douzo	-	Daddy, you take this
petanko shita	-	I stamped them[25]
kutsu itai	-	My shoes hurt
obake kowakunai	-	Ghosts aren't scary / I'm not scared of ghosts
shashin kowai	-	Having photos taken is scary
kami kirei	-	Her hair is pretty

Day 13

Otousan no oishii?	-	Is Daddy's tasty?[26]
mata kuru ka na?	-	I wonder if we will come here again?
ippai haitteru nee	-	There are lots inside, aren't there
omizu haitteru ne	-	There is water in it
taisou no kaado ne	-	It's the exercise card
waratteru yo!	-	He's laughing!
kou ja nai?	-	It's like this, isn't it?

---

[22] '*oneesan*' also means elder sister.
[23] This should be just '*atarashii doresu*'.
[24] '*-you*' and '*-mashou*' mean 'let's', but the speaker is not necessarily included. So '*okiyou*' could also mean 'Let's get you up'.
[25] '*petanko*' or '*pettanko*' usually means 'to crush flat', but as a children's word it can mean 'to stamp'.
[26] The particle '*wa*' is implied: '*Otousan no wa oishii?*'.

Okaasan, A-chan jabajaba shita	- Mummy, A-chan went swimming[27]

Common mistakes

A-chan kore kite kudasai	- Please dress A-chan in this[28]
oide shite	- Come on[29]

Day 14

Otousan, kore kawaii wan-piisu	- Daddy, this is a cute one-piece dress
waa! oishisou da ne!	- Oh! It looks delicious!
A-chan Minnie-chan tabechatta	- A-chan ate Minnie Mouse
tsukenai	- We won't turn it on[30]
kore kashite kita	- I lent this to him[31]

Common mistakes

kareeraisu denakatchatta no	- The curry rice didn't come out[32]

Day 15

hayaku okite	- Get up quickly / Quick, wake up[33]
zembu yatte	- Do all of them
koko oite kudasai	- Please leave it here[34]

---

[27] From '*jabujabu*' (splashing). Both '*jabajaba*' and '*jabujabu*' are used as children's words for swimming. So '*jabajaba suru*' is a bit like 'going splash splash'.
[28] Should be '... *kisete kudasai*' (Please dress me), since '... *kite kudasai*' would mean 'Please wear it'.
[29] Should be just '*oide*'.
[30] '*tsukeru*' and '*tsukenai*' are commonly used for appliances such as lights, television, computer, heater etc.
[31] '*kashite kita*' means 'I went there and lent it', so she probably really just meant '*kashita*' (I lent it).
[32] '*denakatchatta*' should be '*denakatta*' (didn't come out) or '*denakunatchatta*' (stopped coming out).
[33] '*hayaku*' means quickly or early.
[34] The particle '*ni*' is implied.

A-chan ssshh shita	- A-chan went "Sshh!"
hayaku, notte te	- Quick, get on
wakatta?	- Do you understand? / Did you understand?
hayaku okichatta	- She got up early

Common mistakes

A-chan ookii ja nai	- A-chan is not big[35]

Day 16

hai douzo	- Here you go[36]
kore nan darou?	- What is this?[37]
watashi mochitai	- I want to hold it[38]
kagami da ne	- It's a mirror, isn't it
kore A-chan no	- This is A-chan's
Otousan, kore guru tto mawashite	- Daddy, turn this round and round
Otousan, yamete!	- Daddy, stop it!
doite	- Move out the way
Mama pasokon miteru ne	- Mummy is looking at the computer

Day 17

A-chan Disneyland ikitai	- A-chan wants to go to Disneyland
A-chan no ban dakara	- Because it's A-chan's turn
A-chan tsukatteru kara, kore mite	- A-chan is using it, so look at this
mimi souji	- Ear cleaning

---

[35] A-chan placed emphasis on '*ja nai*', because she meant '*ookikunai*' (not big). Without that emphasis the meaning would be the same as '*ookii jan*' (big, isn't it).
[36] This is a slightly different meaning for '*hai douzo*', which was previously seen as 'Okay, go ahead'.
[37] '*darou*' (probably) is informal speech for the neutral/polite '*deshou*' (probably).
[38] '*watashi*' is neutral/polite for 'I / me'.

te aratta -	I washed my hands
atashi -	I / me[39]

Day 18

kore da yo! -	It's this! / It's this one!
yokatta ne -	That's good, isn't it
Okaasan nureteru? -	Is Mummy wet?
kami nureteru no -	Her hair is wet
mite, Okaasan, mite, T-shatsu buruu da -	Look, Mummy, look, the T-shirt is blue
watashi mo muzukashii kara nee -	It's hard for me too, so... you know?[40]

Day 19

yannai -	I won't do it[41]
Otousan, yooguruto taimu da yo! -	Daddy, it's yogurt time![42]
jouzu tabeta -	I ate them well[43]
chotto! -	Please!! (complaining) / Hang on a minute![44]
kore, atashi wa, pinku -	These ones, I'll have the pink one
torechau -	It will come off

Common mistakes

dekinai dakara -	Because I can't do it[45]

Day 20

Mickey Mouse ita yo! -	Mickey Mouse was there!

---

[39] '*atashi*' is feminine speech for '*watashi*' (I / me).
[40] The particle '*ni*' is implied: '*watashi ni mo...*'
[41] A contraction of '*yaranai*' (won't do).
[42] '*taimu*' is a loan-word from 'time' in English.
[43] The particle '*ni*' is implied.
[44] Literally 'A little!', short for '*chotto matte*' (wait a minute).
[45] Should be '*dekinai kara*', since '*da*' and '*dakara*' cannot be used after a verb.

watashi wa kowai yo!	-	I'm scared!
atashi nee...	-	Me, well...
jouzu ne	-	You're good at it, aren't you[46]
sorosoro ikou	-	Let's go now / Let's go soon[47]
kega shichatta	-	I got hurt
watashi mo hairitai	-	I want to go in too
sagashite miyou	-	Let's look for it[48]
itai, itai, tonde ike!	-	Hurt, hurt, fly away![49]

Common mistakes

aruku ja nai	-	I won't walk[50]
aruku dakara	-	Because I'll walk[51]

Day 21

te de yaru	-	I will use my hands[52]
suwarou ka?	-	Shall we sit down?
kakureteru?	-	Is it hiding? / Is it hidden?
tsugi wa orinai no	-	We won't get off at the next one
tatte kudasai	-	Please stand up
genki n natta	-	I feel better now[53]
guru guru mawashite pinku natta	-	I turned it round and round and it went pink[54]
yamete yo!	-	Cut that out! / Stop it![55]

---

[46] '*ne*' used without '*da*' is more common in feminine speech.
[47] '*sorosoro*' means soon, very soon, or now.
[48] '*-te miyou*' means to do something and see.
[49] A standard expression to use when a child has a small scrape.
[50] Should be '*arukanai*'.
[51] Should be '*aruku kara*'.
[52] Literally '*I will do it with my hands*'.
[53] '*ni*' has been contracted to '*n*'.
[54] The particle '*ni*' is implied: '*pinku ni natta*'.
[55] In feminine speech '*yo*' can follow the '*-te*' form.

Day 22

neteru	-	She's lying down
demo okiteru	-	But she's awake
nani?	-	What?
oshikko denakatta	-	Wee didn't come out / No wee came out
kore ja nai	-	It's not this one
are? nai yo!	-	Huh? It's not there!

Day 23

chotto doite kudasai	-	Please move out the way a bit[56]
shimatchatta	-	It closed
A-chan pantsu naru	-	A-chan will start wearing underpants[57]
M-chan pantsu natta	-	M-chan wears underpants now
saa, ikou	-	Come on, let's go

Day 24

tomodachi to asobitai	-	I want to play with my friends
kenka shinai de	-	Don't fight / Don't argue
otete aratte	-	Wash your hands[58]
kagi dekimashita	-	I could unlock it / I was able to unlock it

Common mistakes

Okaasan, ichiban dore ga suki?	-	Mummy, which do you like most?[59]

Day 25

Inai Inai Baa nai	-	The Inai Inai Baa (DVD) is gone

---

[56] If you add a pause here, as in '*chotto, doite kudasai*', the meaning of '*chotto*' changes from 'a bit' to 'Hey!', as in 'Hey! Please move out the way'.
[57] Literally 'A-chan will become underpants'.
[58] '*otete*' is a children's word for '*te*' (hands).
[59] Should be '*ichiban suki na no dore?*' or '*dore ga ichiban suki?*'.

sagashite mite	-	Try looking for it
pantsu haiteru yo	-	I'm wearing underpants[60]
jabajaba suru no	-	We're going to swim
jabajaba, jabajaba, jabajaba!	-	Splash, splash, splash!
jabajaba ikou	-	Let's go swimming
Okaasan toire	-	Mummy is in the toilet
Otousan shawaa shita ne	-	Daddy, you had a shower didn't you
kami yatta?	-	Did you do your hair?

Day 26

kore nee, gacha gacha haitteta	-	This one, it was inside a gacha gacha[61]
purinsesu naritai	-	I want to be a princess
toreta	-	I could reach it / I got it
wasuremono	-	We forgot something[62]
kore piipii shite ii?	-	Can I take this through the checkout counter?[63]
neko-chan daisuki	-	I love pussy cats[64]
osampo desu	-	We are having a walk[65]
kore gomi	-	This is rubbish / This is trash
oekaki shitai	-	I want to draw pictures

---

[60] *'haiteru'* from *'haku'* (to wear below the waist).
[61] The particle *'ni'* is implied.
[62] *'wasuremono'* literally means 'something forgotten'.
[63] *'piipii'* is a children's term for paying at a checkout counter.
[64] Personal pronouns and objects are often omitted, so this sentence structure appears similar to the earlier entry *'A-chan daisuki'* (A-chan loves them). So depending on the context, *'neko-chan daisuki'* could even mean 'Cats love them'.
[65] Prefixing *'o'* to *'sampo'* makes it a children's word.

("**kakikaki**" – the sound of drawing)

Day 27

dame yo!	-	You mustn't do that![66]
Otousan zembu nonda?	-	Did Daddy drink it all?
ima hajimaru yo	-	It will start now
dansu shite	-	Please dance
haitta?	-	Did it go in?
haittenai	-	It's not in there / It hasn't gone in
shuppatsu shinkou!	-	We're off!
Okaasan orita yo	-	Mummy got off
kore yatte miyou ka	-	Shall we try this?

Notes

➢ A-chan now uses many time words, such as '*asa*' (morning), '*ima*' (now), '*atode*' (later) and '*saki ni*' (earlier than).

Day 28

ato wa A-chan	-	The rest are for A-chan
Okaasan, fuite	-	Mummy, wipe it
A-chan atode taberu	-	A-chan will eat later
yoroshiku!	-	Please take care of it / I'll leave it to you then[67]
yoshi!	-	Okay! / All right! / Here we go!
sagashiteru	-	I'm looking for it / I'm searching

---

[66] This is feminine speech since '*yo*' is used without '*da*'.
[67] '*yoroshiku*' has various other meanings, including 'Best regards' and 'Please treat me favorably'.

oishisou! itadakimasu	-	It looks delicious! I will have some[68]
suwatte	-	Please sit
suwatte te	-	Please sit[69]
suwatte kudasai	-	Please sit[70]
asa desu	-	It's morning
A-chan saki ni yomu	-	A-chan will read it first

Day 29

Okaasan, Otousan daijoubu datta	-	Mummy, Daddy was okay[71]
okane irete ii?	-	Can I put the money in?
abunai yo!	-	Look out! / It's dangerous![72]
sugu naosu yo	-	I will fix it straight away

Common mistakes

chiisai ga aru	-	There is a small one[73]

Day 30

ochichatta, abunai!	-	It fell down, look out!
Otousan kitanai	-	Daddy is dirty
sawaranai yo	-	You won't touch it[74]
gochisou sama deshita	-	Thank you for the meal[75]
jampu shiyo	-	Let's jump

---

[68] '*itadakimasu*' is always said before eating.
[69] '*-te te*' makes this literally 'Please be sitting'.
[70] '*kudasai*' makes this more polite.
[71] '*datta*' (was) is the past tense of '*da*' (is).
[72] Previously A-chan put '*desu*' before '*yo*'.
[73] Should be '*chiisai no ga aru*'.
[74] This could also mean 'I won't touch it', but in this case A-chan is using the negative verb form as a command, meaning 'Don't touch it'. In English we might also say 'You don't touch this, okay?'.
[75] This is a standard expression, often shortened to '*gochisou sama*'. '*deshita*' (was) is the past tense of '*desu*' (is).

Two years: Month nine

Day 1

A-chan morechatta	-	A-chan has leaked
kigaete ii?	-	Can I get changed?
kakurembo shita	-	We played hide and seek
Otousan daisuki	-	Daddy loves them[1]
A-chan mo daisuki	-	A-chan loves them too
A-chan mikan tabeta	-	A-chan ate a mandarin
kore desu	-	It's this
asondenai	-	I'm not playing / I haven't played

Common mistakes

chiisai ga ii	-	I want the small one[2]
Otousan itte kite ii?	-	Can I go and see Daddy?[3]

Day 2

boku yomu	-	I'll read it
Papa, omoshiroi nee	-	Daddy, it's interesting isn't it
kore M-chan ga ii tte itta yo	-	M-chan said this was okay[4]
kotchi da yo	-	Over here / This way
mite, kore hippatta	-	Look, I pulled this
hippatchatta	-	I pulled it all / I've gone and pulled it
Otousan wa san-sai	-	Daddy is three years old
shite yo!	-	Do it!

---

[1] This could also mean 'I love Daddy', depending on the context.
[2] Should be '*chiisai no ga ii*'.
[3] Should be '*Otousan ni itte kite ii?*', to avoid sounding like 'Can Daddy go?' or 'Daddy, can I go?'. The '*ni*' could be omitted if '*Otousan*' was a place, like '*kouen*' (park). Another way to say this would be '*Otousan no tokoro itte kite ii?*' (Can I go to where Daddy is?).
[4] '*tte itta*' (written っていった in hiragana) is often used in speech instead '*to itta*'. It can also be pronounced '*te itta*'.

beddo itte kite	-	Go to the bed[5]
osoto ikitai	-	I want to go outside
ikanai	-	I won't go[6]
kigaeru	-	I will change clothes
Papa ikou	-	Daddy let's go
A-chan mou ikko aru yo	-	A-chan has one more
hayaku tsukete	-	Quick, put it on[7]
ikou ka?	-	Shall we go?
Okaasan, A-chan densha ni notta yo	-	Mummy, A-chan went on the train
mou owatchatta	-	It's all finished already
Papa kagami mite	-	Daddy look at the mirror
S-chan kore motteru	-	S-chan has one of these[8]
Cinderella mitai da yo	-	It's like Cinderella[9]
koohii katte ii yo	-	You can buy coffee / You may buy coffee
kimochi ii	-	It feels good[10]
kaze kimochi ii	-	The wind feels nice
ofuro hairanai	-	I won't get in the bath
A-chan saki	-	A-chan first
kore yaritai	-	I want to do this

---

[5] '*kite*' (come) means the instruction is to go to the bed and come back. It doesn't mean 'Go to the bed and stay there' or 'Go to bed'.

[6] This was in response to '*ikitai?*' (Do you want to go?)'. As in English, '*ikanai*' (I won't go) is softer than the more direct '*ikitakunai*' (I don't want to go).

[7] Here A-chan meant to put on clothes, but '*hayaku tsukete*' could also have meant 'Quick, turn it on' (television etc).

[8] '*motteru*' here means 'to possess', from '*motsu*' 'to hold'.

[9] '*mitai*' here means 'to resemble'. Unlike '*mitai*' (want to see), '*mitai*' (to resemble) can be followed by '*da*'.

[10] '*kimochi ii*' (It feels good) is a common expression. The opposite is '*kimochi warui*' (revolting / disgusting).

Common mistakes

hantai te	-	Opposite hand / Other hand[11]

Day 3

banzai!	-	Hooray!
omutsu kaeta deshou?	-	You changed the nappy, right?
hazukashii yo	-	How embarrassing
ao n natta	-	It went blue[12]
nani okotteru no?	-	What are you angry about?
dame deshou!	-	That's bad, right!
nan desu ka?	-	What is it?
minna ni kitenai	-	Not everyone's has arrived yet[13]
mushi ga! mushi ga!	-	A bug...! A bug...![14]
Okaasan yatte mite	-	Mummy please try it
Cinderella to ouji-sama mitai	-	Just like Cinderella and the prince
unchi shiteru	-	I am doing poos
sou da ne	-	That's right
yasashii	-	He's kind
ii ko ii ko	-	Good boy, good boy[15]
ii ko da ne	-	He's a good boy isn't he
ii ko ii ko shita	-	I patted him[16]

---

[11] Should be '*hantai no te*'.
[12] '*ni*' has been contracted to '*n*'.
[13] The context here was while waiting for food at a restaurant.
[14] The full phrase implied is '*mushi ga iru*' (There's a bug).
[15] Although '*ii ko*' means 'good child', it is usually only repeated like this when patting animals.
[16] Children's speech.

Common mistakes

piipii tte itta yo	-	It went ring-ring[17]

Notes

> Although '*deshou*' means 'probably', it is commonly used in informal speech as a question at the end of a phrase to mean 'Right?' or 'Don't you think?'. A-chan also uses it when scolding, as in '*dame deshou!*' (That's bad, right!).

Day 4

koko kowai	-	It's scary here
kami nagai	-	Your hair is long
denki tsukeru	-	I'll put the lights on
mada asonderu	-	I'm still playing
purinsesu asonde	-	Play princesses
supuun de tabenai	-	I won't eat with a spoon / I won't use a spoon
A-chan asonderu	-	A-chan is playing
kurakunatchatta	-	It got dark / It has become dark[18]
kawaii jan	-	Isn't it cute
ii jan!	-	Isn't it good!
chanto kore yatte kudasai yo!	-	Please do this properly![19]

---

[17] '*piipii tte itta yo*' means 'It said ring-ring'. It should be '*piipii tte natta yo*' (It went ring-ring).

[18] Literally 'It became dark'. From '*kurai*' (dark) and '*-natchatta*' (became), which is from '*natta*' (became), which is from '*naru*' (to become). A-chan however simply learned the whole word.

[19] The word order could also be '*kore chanto yatte kudasai yo*'.

dokashite	-	Move it out the way[20]
Okaasan ga yaru	-	Mummy will do it

Notes

> A-chan is starting to use '*ga*' more often, to show the subject of a phrase. Textbooks usually first teach students to add '*wa*' after the subject, but ironically, this can sound childish. For example '*watashi ga...*' is generally better than '*watashi wa...*' unless trying to emphasize '*watashi*' (I / me), for example to draw some kind of contrast.

Day 5

ashi ga!	-	My legs!
makkura n natta	-	It has become pitch dark[21]
doko itte kuru no?	-	Where are you going?
kowakunatchatta	-	I got scared[22]
dakara abunai deshou!	-	See, it's dangerous, right![23]
kore Okaasan no dakara nee	-	This is Mummy's, so...[24]
Okaasan katte kita no, onigiri	-	Mummy bought them, the rice-balls

Day 6

tsuita yo	-	We have arrived
abunai ne, ki o tsukete	-	It's dangerous, be careful[25]
kore Baaba tsukutta?	-	Did Grandma make this?
kawaikunai	-	It's not cute[26]

---

[20] '*dokashite*' (Move it out the way) means to move something, as opposed to '*doite*' (Move out the way).
[21] '*ni*' has been contracted to '*n*'.
[22] This is good use of '*-chatta*' (to do unintentionally).
[23] '*dakara*' (therefore / so) is used here to mean 'See?'.
[24] Implying for example, 'so... you'd better not touch it'.
[25] '*ki o tsukete*' is a common phrase meaning 'Be careful' or 'Take care of yourself'.
[26] As a question, '*kawaikunai?*' would mean 'Isn't it cute?'.

Cinderella deshou!	-	It's Cinderella, right!
Mickey deru?	-	Will Mickey Mouse be on (television)? / Will Mickey Mouse appear?

Common mistakes

hazukashii ja nai	-	I'm not embarrassed[27]

Day 7

suteki deshou?	-	It's lovely, isn't it? / It's lovely, right?
mou ikkai yatte ii?	-	Can I do it again?
oneesan yatteru?	-	Is the young lady doing it?
kore yada	-	I don't like this / I don't want this
terebi hanarete suwatte	-	Sit down away from the television
tsukawanai no	-	I won't use it
atarashii no tsukatte	-	Use the new one[28]
nonde ii no	-	You can drink it
tabenai de	-	Don't eat it
Otousan, gohan desu yo	-	Daddy, it's dinner[29]

Common mistakes

nonde dame	-	You mustn't drink it / Don't drink it[30]

Day 8

dou shiyou?	-	What shall we do?[31]
funjatta	-	I stood on it / I trod on it
sugoi atsui nee	-	It's really hot isn't it
chotto dake	-	Just a little bit
oshiri tataku yo!	-	I'll smack your bottom!

---

[27] Should be '*hazukashikunai*'.
[28] The particle '*o*' is implied: '*atarashii no o tsukatte*'.
[29] A-chan sometimes uses '*desu*' to make a phrase in the polite/neutral level of speech, for example when making an announcement.
[30] Should be '*nondara dame*'.
[31] '*dou*' means 'how' or 'what'.

itai yo!	-	It will hurt! / It hurts!

Day 9

Otousan mo hanabi ikitai tte itta yo	-	Daddy said he wants to go to the fireworks too
tabeyou ka	-	Shall we eat?
karasu kaiteru	-	I'm drawing a crow
kowai desu	-	I'm scared
chotto doite	-	Move out the way a bit
chotto kashite yo	-	Please give/lend it to me for a minute

Common mistakes

iru desu	-	I need it[32]

Day 10

denai	-	It won't come out
denakatta	-	It didn't come out / None came out
Okaasan okitenai	-	Mummy is not awake / Mummy is not up
mou ikko tsukutte ii?	-	Can I make another one?
omutsu kaetai	-	I want to change my nappy
ouchi kaette	-	Go home
ouchi kaeranai	-	I won't go home[33]
nai desu yo	-	There isn't any / There is none / It's all gone
pakupaku shiteru	-	He's munching on it[34]
oyatsu taimu desu yo!	-	It's snack time!

---

[32] '*desu*' cannot follow the plain form of a verb. This should be '*iru*', '*iru n desu*' or '*irimasu*'.

[33] Normally '*ouchi*' means 'your home', since it is the honorific form of '*uchi*' (home). But in children's speech '*ouchi*' can also mean 'my home'.

[34] '*pakupaku shiteru*' (He's munching) is children's speech, but anyone can say '*pakupaku tabeteru*' (He's munching).

chitchai	-	It's tiny[35]

Common mistakes

S-chan ouchi itte kita nee	-	S-chan came to our house, didn't she[36]
ohashi yaru no!	-	I'll use chopsticks![37]

Day 11

beddo orite ii?	-	Can I get off the bed?
A-chan akachan ja nai	-	A-chan isn't a baby
tsukareta	-	I'm tired / I got tired
tsukareteru no	-	I'm tired
miruku nonda	-	I drank milk
chiisakunatchatta	-	It got smaller
ookikunatchatta	-	It got bigger
dekita! dekinai...	-	I could do it! No I couldn't...
hanashite	-	Let go / Let me go[38]

Common mistakes

oishii ja nai	-	It doesn't taste good[39]

Notes

> ➤ '*chiisakunatchatta*' (It got smaller) and '*ookikunatchatta*' (It got bigger) may seem difficult to pronounce, but A-chan learned them from a song.

Day 12

A-chan tsukutta no, zembu	-	A-chan made them, all of them

---

[35] '*chitchia*' (tiny) is from '*chiisai*' (small). Although it is not strictly a children's word, it is a bit like 'wee' or 'teeny weeny' in English.
[36] Should be '*S-chan ouchi kita nee*', since '*itte kita*' means 'went'.
[37] Should be '*ohashi tsukau no!*'.
[38] A-chan knows '*hanashite*' (let go), but not yet '*hanashite*' (speak).
[39] Should be '*oishikunai*'.

kimochi ii deshou?	-	It feels nice, right?
kore chiisakunatchatta	-	This got smaller / This has become smaller
futari notte	-	You two ride on it
kore noritai yo	-	I want to ride on this
konaida M-chan to itte kita no	-	I went with M-chan the other day[40]
M-chan to mita	-	I saw it with M-chan
hitori yatteru yo	-	He is doing it by himself[41]
otetsudai shite	-	Please help me
misemasu	-	I will show you[42]

Common mistakes

kashinai	-	I won't give it to you / I won't lend it to you[43]
torete	-	Get it[44]

Day 13

dare mo inai no?	-	Isn't there anyone here?
dare mo inai	-	There's nobody here
gomen nasai, sumimasen	-	I'm sorry, excuse me
arigatou gozaimasu	-	Thank you[45]
arigatou gozaimashita	-	Thank you[46]
fukifuki	-	Wipey wipey[47]

---

[40] Although '*konaida*' (recently) is a contraction of '*kono aida*', it is written '*ko-naida*' (こないだ), not '*kon-aida*' (こんあいだ).

[41] A-chan always pronounces '*hitori*' as '*shitori*', as it is commonly heard in speech.

[42] This is an example of A-chan using the '*-masu*' form to deliberately sound more polite. The casual form of '*misemasu*' is '*miseru*'.

[43] Should be '*kasanai*'.

[44] Should be '*totte*'.

[45] '*arigatou gozaimasu*' (Thank you) is more polite than '*arigatou*' (Thanks).

[46] The past tense here ('*-mashita*') emphasizes the thanks is for something that has already happened or is completed.

[47] '*fukifuki*' (wipey, wipey) is children's speech.

Two years: Month nine

kayui	-	It itches / It's itchy
kore mo tsunaide	-	Connect this one too

Day 14

mou akechatta no?	-	Did you open it already?
matteru kara nee	-	I'll be waiting, so okay?
motteru kara nee	-	I have it, so okay?
nagechatta	-	I threw it
kinou jabajaba shita yo!	-	We went swimming yesterday!
kyou jabajaba suru?	-	Will we go swimming today?
S-chan to iku?	-	Will we go with S-chan?
S-chan, ippai jabajaba shita no	-	S-chan swam a lot

Day 15

burokku yatteru kara atode omutsu yaru	-	I'm doing blocks so we will do the nappy later
Okaasan, 'shitai desu' tte oshiete ne	-	Mummy, let me know when you want to do it[48]
sou!	-	Right!
minna ochichatta	-	They all fell off[49]
A-chan ga tsuketa yo	-	A-chan put it on / A-chan turned it on / A-chan attached it
kore tabetai	-	I want to eat this
pan tabechatta	-	I ate bread / I ate all the bread

Day 16

kagami minai	-	I won't look in the mirror
waratte	-	Please laugh / Please smile
mada itai	-	It still hurts
A-chan mo iku?	-	Is A-chan going too?
sara aratteru no	-	She's washing the dishes

---

[48] Literally 'tell me "I want to do it"'. *'oshieru'* means 'to teach' or 'to inform'.

[49] *'minna'* means 'everybody' or 'everything'.

tanoshii nee	-	Isn't this fun
youfuku motte kuru ne	-	I'll go and get the clothes / I'll bring the clothes
ii yo! ii!	-	No, it's okay (you don't need to)
shitagi mo nuide?	-	Taking off my underwear too?[50]

Day 17

Otousan mite, omoshiroi yo!	-	Look Daddy, it's funny!
pikapika shiteru yo	-	It's sparkling
ribon mae da yo	-	The ribbon goes at the front
mawatteru yo	-	It's turning around
tsugi wa nani suru?	-	What will we do next?
tsukarechatta	-	I got tired
shashin totte ii?	-	Can I take a photo?

Common mistakes

doko mo ii	-	Anywhere will do / Anywhere is okay[51]

Notes

> A-chan attempts sentences that are beyond her, by leaving out the parts she can't say yet. For example, '*Okaasan... pii to... Mickey Mouse hajimaru*' (Mummy said Mickey Mouse will start when it goes beep).

Day 18

Okaaan, gohan dekita?	-	Mummy, is dinner ready?[52]
yaranai, denki	-	We won't do them, the lights

---

[50] Finishing a question with '*de?*' is as grammatically dubious as the English translation here. It implies part of the sentence was left unsaid, for example '*shitagi mo nuide neru?*' (Will I also take off my underwear to sleep?)
[51] Should be '*doko de mo ii*'.
[52] A-chan already used '*dekiru*' to mean 'can do', but here it means 'to be ready or completed'.

Okaasan yaranai tte itteru	-	Mummy says we won't do them
nombiri shiteru	-	We are taking it easy
koko kara hairu	-	We go in from here[53]

Common mistakes

jouzu dekita	-	You did it well[54]

Day 19

suupu arigato	-	Thank you for the soup[55]
machigattenai yo	-	You are not wrong / It isn't wrong[56]
machigaetenai yo	-	You are not wrong / It isn't wrong[57]
kyou ohirune shimashita	-	I had a nap today[58]
tabete miru?	-	Will you try (to eat) some?[59]

Day 20

kiechatta	-	It went off / It went out[60]
hipparu?	-	Will you pull it?
tatteru	-	I'm standing up
A-chan Happy Birthday utatteru yo	-	A-chan is singing Happy Birthday
Okaasan, dotchi ga suki?	-	Mummy, which one do you like?

Common mistakes

kuma-chan asonde	-	Play with the teddy bear[61]

---

[53] Previously A-chan had used '*kotchi kara hairu*'.
[54] Should be '*jouzu ni dekita*'.
[55] '*arigatou*' (thank you) can be shortened to '*arigato*'.
[56] Literally 'You didn't make a mistake'.
[57] Both '*machigaetenai*' and '*machigattenai*' mean 'You are not wrong', since '*machigaeru*' means the same as '*machigau*' (to be mistaken).
[58] A-chan makes this polite by adding '*o*' to '*hirune*' (nap) and using '*shimashita*' (did) instead of '*shita*' (did).
[59] Literally 'Will you eat it and see?'.
[60] '*kieru*' (to go off) is for lights etc, like '*kesu*' (to turn off).
[61] Should be '*kuma-chan to asonde*'.

Day 21

ima nanji?	-	What time is it?[62]
kore Otousan, kore Okaasan	-	This one is for Daddy, this one is for Mummy
mou iranai	-	I don't want any more
yatta!	-	Yay![63]
A-chan no kachi	-	A-chan won[64]
nanika kikoeteru	-	I can hear something
amai	-	It's sweet
nomitai naa	-	I wish I could drink some
kotchi kara mita	-	I saw from through here
tasukete tte itteru	-	He is saying "Help"

Common mistakes

atsui ja nai	-	It's not hot[65]

Day 22

A-chan machigaechatta	-	A-chan made a mistake / A-chan did it wrong
kyou konderu nee	-	It's crowded today, isn't it
mou ikko aru	-	There is one more
miyou?	-	Shall we watch it? / Shall we take a look?[66]
kore tsukau?	-	Will you use this?
kaban no naka haitteta yo	-	It was inside the bag[67]
mada aru deshou?	-	There are more, right?
gohan mo suki	-	I like rice too[68]
kore de ii no	-	This will do

---

[62] Literally 'What time is it now?'.
[63] Literally 'We did it!'.
[64] Literally 'A-chan's victory / win'.
[65] Should be '*atsukunai*'.
[66] '*miyou?*' (Shall we watch?) is equivalent to '*miyou ka?*'
[67] '*naka*' means inside.
[68] '*gohan*' can mean either 'cooked rice' or 'meal'.

Day 23

asa n natta	-	It's morning[69]
nonde ii?	-	Can I drink it?
zembu suki ja nai	-	I don't like all of them[70]
minna tabeteru	-	Everyone is eating
mada chiisai desu	-	I'm still small
san-sai ni naru	-	I will turn three years old[71]
oekaki shiyou ka?	-	Shall we draw pictures?
A-chan ga tsuketeru	-	A-chan is putting them on
mada kurai yo	-	It's still dark
oshitai	-	I want to push it
tasukete!	-	Help!
nenne shinai to	-	I have to sleep
nenne shinai to dame	-	I have to sleep[72]
kore yarou ka?	-	Shall we do this?
detenai desu	-	It hasn't come out[73]

Common mistakes

kutsu hakete	-	Put your shoes on[74]
kuruma norinai	-	I won't go in the car[75]

Day 24

okawari!	-	Another helping!
okawari kudasai!	-	Another helping please!

---

[69] Literally 'It has become morning'. '*ni*' has been contracted to '*n*'.
[70] As in the English, it can be unclear whether this means '*zembu ga suki ja nai*' (I don't like any of them), or '*zembu wa suki ja nai*' (I don't like all of them, but I like some of them).
[71] Literally 'I will become three years old'.
[72] '*dame*' literally means 'no good'.
[73] '*desu*' makes this a bit more polite, equivalent to '*detemasen*' (hasn't come out).
[74] Should be '*kutsu haite*'.
[75] Should be '*kuruma noranai*'.

okawari suru no, Okaasan!	-	I'll have another helping, Mummy!
Otousan kigaeta	-	Daddy has changed clothes
kono naka haitteru	-	It's inside here
zembu tabeta	-	I ate it all / I ate them all
Otousan, kuruma ga kuru yo	-	Daddy, a car is coming
daisuki!	-	I love them! / I love her!
sugoi daisuki!	-	I really love them[76]
suteki na doresu	-	It's a lovely dress[77]
arigato tte shitteru?	-	Do you know 'arigato' (thanks)?
pan ochita	-	The bread fell down

Day 25

A-chan ga eranda	-	A-chan chose it
onigiri setto zembu tabechatta	-	I ate all the rice-balls set meal
okotteru	-	I'm angry
me o tsubutte asobou	-	Let's play with our eyes closed[78]
A-chan no tanjoubi tsugi da yo	-	A-chan's birthday is next
byouin ikanai	-	I won't go to the hospital

Notes

> A-chan incorrectly adds '*datte*' to some sentences:

zerii tabetai datte	-	I want to eat jelly[79]
ochita datte	-	It fell down[80]

---

[76] '*sugoi daisuki*' (really love) should actually be '*sugoku daisuki*', but '*sugoi*' is often used like this in speech. Another example is '*sugoi ii*' (really good), which should be '*sugoku ii*'.
[77] A-chan uses particle '*na*' here. She does not know which adjectives take '*na*', but simply imitates what she has heard.
[78] Literally 'Closing eyes, let's play'.
[79] Should be just '*zerii tabetai*'.
[80] Should be just '*ochita*'.

Day 26

ikou yo!	-	Let's go!
kore omoshiroi yo!	-	This is interesting! / This is fun!
mata dete kichatta	-	It came out again
hai, dekimashita!	-	Okay, all done!
chotto dake, wakatta?	-	Just a little, understand?

Day 27

Okaasan no tanjoubi yatta	-	We did Mummy's birthday
fuu shita nee	-	We blew on them, didn't we[81]
mitai? miyou ka?	-	Do you want to see it? Shall we watch it?
koko notte ii?	-	Can I get on here?

Day 28

oneesan mo kuru	-	The young lady will come too
Otousan no pajama, dotchi ga ii?	-	Daddy which pajamas do you want?
akete ii yo tte itta	-	He said I could open it / He said it was okay to open it
kyou NanDeemo da yo	-	Today is NanDeemo
chotto itakatta	-	It hurt a bit
miruku tsuiteru	-	There's milk on it / You have milk on you

Day 29

kore mo omocha	-	This is a toy too
A-chan wa tsukau	-	A-chan will use it[82]
atode tsukau	-	I will use it later
datte tsukawanai	-	Well because, I won't use it

---

[81] '*fuu shita*' is children's speech.
[82] '*wa*' here implies a contrast, such as 'Maybe you won't use it, but A-chan will'.

mou dame yo	-	You mustn't do that anymore[83]
nenasai!	-	Go to sleep!
A-chan aketa	-	A-chan opened it
Mickey inakatta nee	-	Mickey Mouse wasn't there, was he?
goji da yo!	-	It's 5 o'clock![84]
makkura tte shitteru?	-	Do you know 'makkura' (pitch dark)?

Day 30

Okaasan yaranai, A-chan dake	-	Mummy won't do it, only A-chan
Minnie-chan yonderu yo	-	Minnie Mouse is calling
kono naka haitchatta	-	It went in here
mou daijoubu ne	-	It's okay now, isn't it
ouchi kaeru	-	I'm going home
boku mo yaritai	-	I want to do it too
denki wa?	-	What about the lights?
ugoita	-	It moved
koronjatta	-	I fell over
Otousan aruite	-	Daddy, (please) walk
saki ni itte	-	Please go on ahead
itte kite	-	Off you go

Day 31

Otousan to itte kite	-	Go with Daddy
A-chan motte kuru	-	A-chan will bring it
motte kita yo	-	I brought it
M-chan hikouki de kaette kuru	-	M-chan will come back on a plane
kabutteru	-	She's wearing it (on her head)
minna oide oide!	-	Everyone, come on, come on!
sugoi ase kaiteru, Otousan	-	You've sweated a lot, Daddy
tamago o tsukuru yo	-	I will make eggs

---

[83] Literally 'It's already bad', since '*mou*' means 'already'.
[84] A-chan cannot yet tell the time, but she knows it is called '5 o'clock' when the neighbourhood chimes ring.

Common mistakes

chiisai yatte ii?	-	Can I do it quietly?[85]
keshinai de	-	Don't turn it off[86]

---

[85] A-chan is trying to say the words *'chiisaku shite ii?'* (Can I turn it down?), but actually means *'shizuka ni shite ii?'* (Can I do it quietly?).
[86] Should be *'kesanai de'*.

Two years: Month ten

Day 1

doushite?	-	Why?
Papa asagohan o tsukuru	-	Daddy will make breakfast
A-chan no asagohan mo tsukuru	-	He will make A-chan's breakfast too
chotto abunakatta	-	It was a bit dangerous / It was a close call

Day 2

S-chan to asonda	-	I played with S-chan
reezun kudasai yo!	-	Give me some raisins please!
hito ni yaranai de ne	-	Don't do that to people, okay?
Okaasan kore dekinai nee	-	Mummy can't do this, can she
Okaasan dekinai, kore	-	Mummy can't do this[1]

Notes

> Many children use 'choudai' instead of 'kudasai'. For adults 'choudai' is feminine speech.

Day 3

A-chan wa pinku to pinku	-	A-chan will have the pink one and the pink one
sugoi tsumetai nee	-	It's really cold (to the touch) isn't it
sugoi attakai nee	-	It's really warm isn't it[2]
chotto atsui	-	It's a bit hot
nee?	-	Right?

Day 4

ikinasai!	-	Go!
hipparanai de ne	-	Don't pull it okay?

---

[1] Adding the subject at the end of the phrase is very conversational, but will sound silly if overused.

[2] *'attakai'* is a contraction of *'atatakai'* (warm).

kinai desu	-	I won't wear it
a!	-	Ah!
Okaasan, Otousan ga kaette kita yo	-	Mummy, Daddy has come home[3]

Day 5

todokanai	-	It doesn't reach / I can't reach[4]
funderu yo	-	You're standing on it / You're treading on it
iku yo!	-	Here we go![5]
Papa katte kitenai deshou?	-	Daddy didn't go and buy it, did he?
miruku koboreru	-	The milk will spill
nagashitai	-	I want to flush it[6]
nagashite ii?	-	Can I flush it?

Day 6

datte konderu kara	-	Well because, it's crowded
zembu konderu	-	They are all crowded
koko de nenne shite	-	Sleep here
nande sugoi?	-	Why is it amazing? / What's so amazing?
kore mo suppai	-	This one is sour too
sorosoro owaru	-	It will finish soon
ima odotteru kara	-	Because I'm dancing now
atama hairu ka na?	-	I wonder if my head will fit in?
hayaku!	-	Hurry!

---

[3] '*kaette kita*' (returned) is like '*kaetta*' (returned), but emphasizes returning to where the speaker is.

[4] '*todokanai*' is from '*todoku*' meaning 'to reach' or 'to be delivered'.

[5] This is a different meaning to '*iku yo*' used previously to mean 'I'm going'.

[6] '*nagasu*' means 'to drain / pour / wash away', but A-chan uses it here to refer to flushing the toilet.

Common mistakes

nani haittenai yo	-	There is nothing inside it[7]
hitotsu nai	-	There is only one[8]

Notes

➢ Children often confuse words as they are learning them, and can continue to use a wrong word no matter how many times someone corrects them. In A-chan's case, she often says 'kakurembo' (hide and seek) instead of 'sakurambo' (cherry). She also says 'kakurembo' (hide and seek) instead of 'kakigoori' (shaved ice).

Day 7

ja, kore yaro?	-	Then, shall we do this?[9]
mite, sugoi yo!	-	Look, it's amazing! / Wow, look at this!
chanto tabeteru yo	-	I'm eating properly
suwattara?	-	Why don't you sit down? / How about sitting down?[10]
suwattetara?	-	Why don't you sit down? / How about sitting down?[11]

Common mistakes

ikitai ja nai	-	I don't want to go[12]
mada itakatta	-	It still hurts[13]

---

[7] Should be '*nani mo haittenai yo*'.
[8] Should be '*hitotsu shika nai*'.
[9] '*yaro*' is a contraction of '*yarou*' (Let's do).
[10] '*-tara*' is often used in informal speech when suggesting someone do something.
[11] A contraction of '*suwatte itara?*', which literally means 'Why don't you be sitting down?'.
[12] Should be '*ikitakunai*'.
[13] Should be '*mada itai*' (It still hurts), since '*mada itakatta*' would mean 'It still hurt (past tense)'.

Day 8

yukkuri nonde	-	Drink it slowly
atashi kimeta	-	I have decided
kore dekiru?	-	Can you do this?
hora, mite	-	See, look

Day 9

Kitty-chan ga ippai	-	There are lots of Hello Kitty ones
dame desu	-	That's bad
Okaasan mukae ni kita	-	Mummy came to pick me up
A-chan da yo!	-	It's A-chan![14]
dashitenai	-	I haven't spat it out

Day 10

dou yatte hairu?	-	How can we get in? / How can it go in?
ookikunatta no	-	It got bigger[15]
nakushichatta	-	We lost it[16]
hai, torimasu!	-	Okay, I'll take the picture!

Day 11

takai yo!	-	It's high!
gambare! gambare!	-	You can do it! You can do it!
pantsu ga hazukashii	-	Underpants are embarrassing
K-chan waratta	-	K-chan laughed

Day 12

tabechau yo!	-	I will eat it! / I will eat you!
ashi kurokunatchatta	-	My legs turned black
A-chan ocha nomitai desu	-	A-chan wants to drink tea

---

[14] A-chan still uses '*-chan*' after her own name.
[15] Previously she used only '*ookikunatchatta*' (It got bigger).
[16] This is good use of '*-chatta*' (to do unintentionally).

atode ii yo	- Later is okay / You can do it later[17]
aisukuriimu tabeta nee	- We ate ice-cream, didn't we?
yukkuri tabete	- Eat slowly

("*pakupaku*" – the sound of eating)

Common mistakes

shinkansen ni notte, shinai to, iku n desu	- We have to go by shinkansen[18]

Day 13

oishii, T-kun?	- Is it tasty, T-kun?
odorou yo!	- Let's dance!
A-chan no Papa!	- It's A-chan's Daddy!
tsugi wa S-chan yo	- Next is S-chan[19]
kite ne	- Come, okay?
fuite kudasai	- Please wipe it
fu fu fu fu	- Hee hee hee hee (giggling sound)

Day 14

Okaasan, hora, asa ni natta	- Mummy, see, it's now morning
tabenai?	- Won't you eat some?
kono kuruma mita nee	- We saw this car, didn't we

---

[17] '*atode*' is usually considered a single word, but is actually '*ato de*'. So an extra particle '*de*' is not needed as it is in phrases like '*kore de ii*' (This will do).
[18] Literally this says 'We will take the bullet train, we have to, and go there'. It should be '*shinkansen ni notte ikanai to*' or '*shinkansen ni noranai to ikenai*' to mean 'We have to go by shinkansen'.
[19] This is feminine speech with '*yo*' instead of '*da yo*'.

zembu aru desho?	-	They are all there, right?[20]
A-chan ga yatte ii?	-	Can A-chan do it? / May A-chan do it?
sugoi oishii ne	-	It's so tasty, isn't it
T-kun notta ne, ouma-san	-	T-kun rode on it didn't he, on the horse
ouma-san tabeta nee	-	The horse ate it, didn't he[21]
A-chan mo tabetai	-	A-chan wants to eat some too

Day 15

Otousan, onaka miechatta yo!	-	Daddy, we can see your tummy![22]
osampo iku no	-	We're going for a walk
A-chan yatchatta no?	-	Did A-chan (accidentally) do it?
kore yaru?	-	Will you do this? / Shall we do this?
mada A-chan yatteru	-	A-chan is still doing it
kotchi ga ii	-	I want this one
sou yo	-	That's right[23]
kore yarou yo, Papa!	-	Let's do this, Daddy!

Common mistakes

omizu nominai	-	I won't drink water[24]
ookii da yo!	-	It's big![25]

Day 16

hee?	-	Really?
A-chan nenne shiteru kara oyasumi nasai	-	A-chan is sleeping, so goodnight

---

[20] '*desho*' is a contraction of '*deshou*' (Right?).
[21] Without a particle to show whether this is '*ouma-san ga tabeta*' (The horse ate it) or '*ouma-san o tabeta*' (I ate the horse), we can only guess from the context.
[22] '*miechatta*' literally means 'Could see (unintentionally)'.
[23] This is feminine speech with '*yo*' instead of '*da yo*'.
[24] Should be '*omizu nomanai*'.
[25] Should be '*ookii yo*'.

isshoni yaro?	-	Shall we do it together?
doushite shinai no?	-	Why won't you do it?
ashi ga dete kichatta	-	My legs have come out / My legs are sticking out

Day 17

kore wa chaahan da yo	-	This is fried rice
chotto yatte ii?	-	Can I do this a bit?
hitotsu douzo	-	Help yourself to one
Shima-chan miyou ka?	-	Shall we watch Shima-chan?[26]
nenne shinai de	-	Don't go to sleep
kowarechatta, megane	-	They're all broken, your glasses[27]
zenzen unchi ga detenai	-	I haven't done any poos at all

Common mistakes

yomiyou yo	-	Let's read[28]
yomiyou ka?	-	Shall we read?[29]

Day 18

ja, okiyou	-	Then, let's get up
kore yaranai yo	-	I won't do this
zettai yaranai	-	I definitely won't do it[30]
zettai tabenai de	-	You absolutely mustn't eat it[31]
S-chan taberu ka na?	-	I wonder if S-chan will eat it?

---

[26] Shimajiro (Shima-chan) is a tiger character popular with pre-schoolers.
[27] The usual word order would be '*megane kowarechatta*' (Your glasses are all broken).
[28] Should be '*yomou yo*'.
[29] Should be '*yomou ka?*'.
[30] The particle '*ni*' is implied: '*zettai ni yaranai*'.
[31] The particle '*ni*' is implied: '*zettai ni tabenai de*'.

hitotsu ga ii? zembu iru?	-	Is one enough? Or do you want them all?[32]

Day 19

A-chan hitori de iku	-	A-chan will go by herself
sou yatte yatte, goshi goshi	-	Do it like that, and rub-rub
tabemono da yo	-	It's food
M-chan ikitai n datte	-	M-chan says she wants to go
jibun ni aru desho?	-	You have your own, right?
fuu shite kudasai	-	Please blow on it
supuun ga nai	-	There is no spoon / I don't have a spoon
mou yaranai	-	I won't do it anymore
asa nattenai	-	It isn't morning yet

Common mistakes

hitori dekiru no	-	I can do it by myself[33]
hitori dekita no	-	I did it by myself[34]

Day 20

A-chan saki da yo	-	A-chan goes first
Otousan oinori yatte	-	Daddy, do prayers / Daddy, say grace
sugoi desu ka?	-	Is it amazing?
mou ikkai deru yo	-	It will come out again
dechatta	-	It came out
tsunaide	-	Please hold hands[35]
suzushii	-	It's cool (weather)
datte asobanai	-	Well, because you won't play

---

[32] 'Or' is implied between the two phrases here. In Japanese questions with multiple choices can be asked as separate consecutive sentences.
[33] Should be '*hitori de dekiru no*'.
[34] Should be '*hitori de dekita no*'.
[35] Should be '*te tsunaide*' or '*te o tsunaide*', but just '*tsunaide*' is okay if clear from context.

Day 21

orinai	-	I won't get down / I won't get off
ii yo tte itta?	-	Did she say it's okay?
tori ni kite	-	Come and get it
tori ni ikou yo	-	Let's go and get it
kimeta?	-	Have you decided?
mou kichatta	-	They're here already[36]
zembu tabenai	-	I won't eat them all / I can't eat it all

Common mistakes

kore doite	-	Move this[37]

Day 22

A-chan no pantsu aratteru no	-	She's washing A-chan's underpants
kore mae da yo	-	This is the front
kore fuusen datta	-	This was a balloon
motte kitenai	-	I didn't bring it
oyoide	-	Please swim
mukou itte	-	Go over there

Day 23

kore Okaasan to A-chan to yatta ne	-	Mummy and A-chan did this together
doresu kiyou	-	Let's wear the dress[38]
Otousan, asagohan tsukurou yo	-	Daddy, let's make breakfast
nenne suru n datte, Minnie-chan	-	She says she will sleep, Minnie Mouse

---

[36] A-chan previously used '*kichatta*' (wore) from '*kiru*' (to wear), but here it is '*kichatta*' (came) from '*kuru*' (to come).
[37] Should be '*kore dokashite*'.
[38] The '*-you*' form is used here to refer only to the speaker. So although '*kiyou*' literally means 'Let's wear', only A-chan will wear the dress.

okotchau yo, nee?	-	I will get angry, won't I?[39]
kore mo daisuki	-	I love this one too
Otousan mo hashirou	-	Daddy, you run too[40]
Otousan mo suwarou	-	Daddy, you sit too
zembu yaranai de ne	-	Don't do all of them, okay?

Day 24

hora, Shima-chan!	-	Look, it's Shima-chan!
oshikko shite ii?	-	Can I do wees?
iru? iranai ka	-	Do you want it? You don't[41]
jaa nee, Shima-chan, baibai	-	See you later Shima-chan, bye bye
hon totte kita	-	I went and got the book / I fetched the book
ja jaan!	-	Ta-dah!

Day 25

nonjau	-	I'll drink it / I'll drink it all
watashi ga yaru yo	-	I will do it
osokatta nee	-	It was late wasn't it? / It was slow wasn't it? / You were late, weren't you?
itte kuru?	-	Will you go?
sugoi, atashi	-	I'm amazing / Wow, look at me
A-chan sugoi	-	A-chan is amazing / Wow, look at A-chan
shimeru?	-	Will you close it? / Shall we close it?[42]
shimete	-	Close it

---

[39] '*nee?*' can be used by itself like this, as a request for confirmation.
[40] The '*-you*' form is used here on behalf of someone else. So although '*hashirou*' literally means 'Let's run', A-chan might not intend to run herself.
[41] '*ka*' here is pronounced in a flat tone that indicates this is not a question, similar to 'Do you want it? Oh, don't you'.
[42] Although the '*-ru*' verb form in a question literally means 'Will we?', it is often used to mean 'Shall we?', like '*-you*'.

hayaku, hayaku	-	Hurry, hurry
hairanai de	-	Don't go in
ikanai de	-	Don't go
saki A-chan yaru	-	A-chan will do it first

Day 26

dekitenai ne	-	It's not ready, is it
iranai desu	-	I don't want it / I don't need it
saki douzo	-	Please go ahead first
tsugi A-chan no ban da yo!	-	Next is A-chan's turn!
mata A-chan no kao da yo!	-	There is A-chan's face again!

Common mistakes

tsukamaete	-	Grab hold / Hold on[43]

Day 27

suwatte matteru no	-	He is sitting and waiting[44]
Okaasan wa atode kuru	-	Mummy will come later
Papa no, aketa	-	I opened Daddy's one[45]
are wa?	-	What about that one?[46]
gohan ni kakete	-	Put it on the rice
Papa wa onigiri daisuki ja nai deshou?	-	Daddy doesn't love rice-balls, right?[47]
oishikatta?	-	Did it taste good?
tabeta?	-	Did you eat it?
A-chan nomitai!	-	A-chan wants to drink some!
koborechatta	-	It spilled

---

[43] '*tsukamaete*' means 'Catch him'. A-chan meant '*tsukamatte*' (Hold on) or '*tsukande*' (Hold on).
[44] This is an example of using the '*-te*' verb form to join phrases.
[45] The particle '*o*' is implied: '*Papa no o aketa*'.
[46] '*are*' here means 'that over there'.
[47] As in the English, '*suki ja nai*' (doesn't like) would be better here than '*daisuki ja nai*' (doesn't love), which sounds childish.

taihen!	-	That's terrible! / That's awful! / Oh no!
fuichau?	-	Will you wipe it?

Common mistakes

hakechau	-	I will wear them / I will put them on (trousers etc)[48]
kore mo kakete	-	Put it on this too[49]
mise ni katte kita	-	I bought it at the shop[50]

Day 28

Papa, otetsudai shite	-	Daddy, help me / Daddy, give me some help
omutsu de shite ii?	-	Can I do it in my nappy?
atashi mise de katte kita no	-	I bought it at the shop
Santa-san kikoeteru	-	I can hear Santa
Otousan oshikko tatte dekiru	-	Daddy can do wees standing up
A-chan suwatte dekiru	-	A-chan can do it sitting down
nagasanai de ne	-	Don't flush it, will you
nani mo shitenai yo	-	I'm not doing anything / I haven't done anything

Common mistakes

kigaerou	-	Let's change clothes / Let's get dressed[51]

Day 29

chigau yo ne	-	It's wrong, isn't it
Otousan, kore jibun de dekiru	-	Daddy, I can do this by myself
A-chan jibun de dekiru no, kore	-	A-chan can do it by herself, this one

---

[48] A-chan was trying to say the word '*haichau*' (accidentally wear), but really meant simply '*haku*' (I will wear them).
[49] Should be '*kore ni mo kakete*' (Put it on this too), since '*kore mo kakete*' would mean 'Put this on too'.
[50] Should be '*mise de katte kita*'.
[51] Should be '*kigaeyou*'.

sawaranai de!	-	Don't touch it! / Don't touch me!
kou yatte, kou yatte...	-	Do it like this, and like this...[52]

Day 30

sorosoro kaerimasu	-	We will go home soon
doumo arigatou gozaimasu	-	Thank you very much
mite te ne	-	Please watch it / Please look at it[53]
kireteru	-	It's snapped / It's broken off
ofuro hairitai	-	I want to get in the bath

Common mistakes

ofuro oriru	-	I will get out the bath[54]

---

[52] Previously A-chan has used '*kou yatte*' (Do it like this), but here she is joining phrases using the '-*te*' verb form.

[53] Literally '*mite te*' means 'be watching it'. This has more of a feeling of 'Stay and watch it' than just '*mite*' (watch it).

[54] Should be '*ofuro deru*'.

Two years: Month eleven

Day 1

dore ka naa?	-	I wonder which one?
ja, asobu	-	Then, we'll play
Otousan taberu, koori?	-	Daddy will you eat some ice?[1]
taberu ka naa?	-	I wonder whether he will eat them?
hanabi miru?	-	Will you watch fireworks?[2]
ikanai yo	-	I won't go
denki tsukete	-	Turn the lights on

Day 2

Okaasan wa shinshitsu ni iru	-	Mummy is in the bedroom
ashi ga itakatta	-	My feet hurt (past tense) / It hurt my feet
gomen nasai tte itte	-	Say sorry
shashin totte ne	-	Take a photo, won't you
ima tsukau	-	I will use it now
oniisan yatchatta	-	The young man did it
kande yo	-	Bite it
kande kudasai	-	Please bite it
Mickey ga tsukau	-	Mickey Mouse will use it

Notes

> A-chan uses 'yaru' (do) and 'suru' (do) interchangeably, although 'yaru' is more casual and has other meanings including 'to kill', 'to give to inferiors or animals' and 'to have sex'.

Day 3

Okaasan to ofuro haitteru	-	I'm having a bath with Mummy

---

[1] The usual word order would be *'Otousan koori taberu?'*.
[2] A-chan incorrectly pronounces *'hanabi'* (fireworks) as *'hanami'* which means 'cherry blossom viewing'.

Okaasan to hon yonderu	-	I'm reading a book with Mummy
a sou ka?	-	Oh, really? / Is that so?[3]
yoshi, gambarou	-	Okay, let's do our best
byouin no sensei naoseru tte itta	-	The doctor at the hospital said he can fix it[4]
NanDeemo mo ashita da yo	-	NanDeemo is tomorrow too
chigau yo, neko-chan ja nai	-	No that's wrong, I'm not a pussy cat

Common mistakes

A-chan wanchan shita yo	-	A-chan made a noise like a dog[5]
A-chan zembu miruku tabeta no	-	A-chan drank all the milk[6]

Day 4

atteru	-	That's right / That's correct
kore ga ii?	-	Is this one okay?
te de tabenai	-	You shouldn't eat it with your hands[7]
supuun de yaru no yo	-	You do it with a spoon
nugu	-	I will undress / I'll take it off (clothes)
sore mo daijoubu	-	That is okay too
uragaeshi ni natchatta	-	It went inside out
kichau	-	It's coming
mou kita yo	-	It's here already / It's here now
juusu katte ikou?	-	Shall we get some juice on the way?
erebeetaa de ikou	-	Let's take the elevator
mae mite	-	Watch where you're going[8]
datte, A-chan itchau yo	-	Well, because A-chan is going
chotto dake juusu nomou ne	-	Let's drink just a little juice

---

[3] '*sou ka?*' (Really?) is often used rhetorically.
[4] This could also mean 'They said the doctor at the hospital can fix it'.
[5] Should be '*A-chan wanchan no mane shita yo*'.
[6] Should be '*nonda*' (drank), not '*tabeta*' (ate).
[7] Literally 'You don't eat it with your hands'.
[8] Literally 'Look front'.

Two years: Month eleven

Otousan nugitai ne	-	Daddy wants to undress
araeba ochiru	-	It will come out in the wash[9]

Common mistakes

nugita	-	I undressed[10]
nugite ii?	-	Can I take it off (clothes)?[11]

Day 5

nakatta kara	-	Because there weren't any
sorosoro san-sai ni narimasu	-	I will be three years old soon
hana mae dakara	-	The flower goes at the front, so...
kore isshoni tabeyou ka?	-	Shall we eat this together?
kiiteru no?	-	Are you listening?
kiite n no?	-	Are you listening?[12]
nani yatteru no?	-	What are you doing?
nani yatte n no?	-	What are you doing?
A-chan seki ga deru kara shiiru haru no	-	A-chan will put stickers on because she has a cough
Otousan mo ofuro haitta	-	Daddy had a bath too
kore dare no?	-	Whose is this?

Common mistakes

yada deshou?	-	It's awful, right?[13]

Day 6

mite mo ii yo	-	You can watch
Okaasan mo mite mo ii yo	-	Mummy can watch too

---

[9] Literally 'If you wash it, it will come out'. A-chan simply memorized this phrase, and cannot yet make or understand other examples of the '-eba' (if) verb form.
[10] Should be '*nuida*'.
[11] Should be '*nuide ii?*'.
[12] '*-n no?*' is extremely casual, and may indicate anger or scolding.
[13] Should be '*yada ne?*' or '*iya deshou?*'.

atode!	-	Later!
mizu owatchau yo	-	The water will finish / The water will stop
A-chan pan daisuki	-	A-chan loves bread
motte te kudasai	-	Please hold it
Otousan motte	-	Daddy, you hold it
maa ii, tabete	-	Well okay, eat it
zembu tabeta?	-	Did you eat it all?
erai!	-	Great! / Well done!
Otousan hayakatta nee	-	Daddy was quick, wasn't he
kore Otousan wakaru ka ne?	-	I wonder whether Daddy understands this?[14]
Otousan no te kirei?	-	Are Daddy's hands clean?
Minnie-chan iru?	-	Do we need Minnie Mouse?[15]
kite, kite	-	Come on, come on
kite yo!	-	Come on!

Common mistakes

chigau desu	-	That's wrong[16]

Day 7

takusan da yo	-	Lots of them
are mo kirei	-	That one is pretty too
omata fuita?	-	Did you wipe your crotch?[17]
oshikko dete	-	Come out, wees
ouchi dakara peropero shite ii no?	-	We are at home, so can I lick it?

---

[14] '*ka ne?*' (I wonder) often anticipates a more positive reply than '*ka?*', while '*ka na?*' (I wonder) is more neutral and can also be used when talking to yourself.

[15] '*iru*' here means 'to need', not 'to be'.

[16] Should be '*chigau*' or '*chigaimasu*', although people do actually say '*chigau desu*'.

[17] '*mata*' means 'crotch' or 'groin'. The '*o*' is honorific, and can sound childish in casual speech.

kore A-chan yaru	-	A-chan will do this
kore A-chan miru no	-	A-chan will watch this
Otousan ga hirotte kureta?	-	Did Daddy pick it up for me?[18]
mata kuru yo	-	She will come back / She will come again
naoseru ka na?	-	I wonder whether they can fix it?
uragaeshi natteru	-	It's inside out[19]
kyoukai no kami-sama naoseru ka naa?	-	I wonder whether God from church can cure you?

Common mistakes

naka ni haittenai	-	There's nothing inside[20]

Day 8

owattenai	-	It's not finished
kuro to shiro	-	Black and white
yasashii hito	-	What a kind person / He's a kind person [21]
kore wa ii?	-	Is this okay?
kore wa ii nee	-	This is okay, isn't it
ii deshou?	-	It's okay, right?
naitenai	-	I'm not crying
kashite ii?	-	Can I lend it to her?
kashite ii desu ka?	-	May I lend it to her?
irete ii?	-	Can I put it in?
irete	-	Put it in
orite	-	Get off
wasureta	-	I forgot
sugoi atsukatta nee	-	It was really hot, wasn't it

---

[18] '*-te kureta*' means 'for me'.
[19] The particle '*ni*' is implied.
[20] Should be '*naka ni nani mo haittenai*' or just '*nani mo haittenai*'.
[21] A-chan always pronounces '*hito*' as '*shito*', as it is commonly heard in speech.

ii ko ii ko shite ageteru yo	-	He's saying 'good boy, good boy' / He is petting it
mada ame futteru	-	It's still raining
Otousan dame da nee	-	Daddy is no good, is he
Okaasan no akachan kawaikunatta nee	-	The mother's baby is so cute now, isn't she?[22]

Common mistakes

ouchi mo aru	-	We have one at home[23]
okotchattenai	-	I'm not angry[24]

Notes

➢ When replying in the negative to a question that uses the '*-ta?*' form, you can use either '*-nakatta*' (didn't) or '*-tenai*' (haven't). A-chan mostly uses '*-tenai*'. Here are some examples:

shita? (Did you?)	-	*shita* (I did); *shinakatta* (I didn't); *shitenai* (I haven't)
owatta? (Is it finished?)	-	*owatta* (It finished); *owaranakatta* (It didn't finish); *owattenai* (It hasn't finished)
mita? (Did you see it?)	-	*mita* (I saw it); *minakatta* (I didn't see it); *mitenai* (I haven't seen it)
naita? (Did you cry?)	-	*naita* (I cried); *nakanakatta* (I didn't cry); *naitenai* (I haven't cried)

Day 9

ireta?	-	Did you put it in?
ireta no, gohan?	-	Did you put it in, the rice?
oto ga shita	-	It made a noise / There was a noise
me ni haitchatta	-	It went in my eye

---

[22] '*kawaikunatta*' literally means 'became cute'.
[23] Should be '*ouchi ni mo aru*'.
[24] Should be '*okottenai*'.

Okaasan kyou nani suru no?	-	Mummy, what will we do today?
omizu tomatchau	-	The water will stop
denwa da yo	-	It's the phone / You have a call
NanDeemo itte kitenai	-	I haven't been to NanDeemo

Day 10

Kitty-chan ga haitchatta	-	Hello Kitty went in
A-chan kayui	-	A-chan is itchy
kayukunai yo	-	It doesn't itch / I'm not itchy
kotchi oite te kudasai	-	Please leave it here
okao ga mienakatta	-	I couldn't see your face
tsukurou ka?	-	Shall I make it?
okiyou ka?	-	Shall we get up?
A-chan kesu yo	-	A-chan will turn it off
Otousan no gohan tsukuru?	-	Shall I make Daddy's dinner? / Are you going to make Daddy's dinner?

Day 11

minna nete kara Okaasan mukai ni kuru	-	Mummy comes to get me after everyone is asleep[25]
tsukatte kudasai	-	Please use it
asonde ii yo	-	You can play
demo tsukawanai de kudasai	-	But please don't use it
A-chan Otousan no gohan tsukuru kara matte te ne	-	A-chan will make Daddy's dinner so wait, okay?
ocha iru?	-	Do you want tea?
ocha iru ne	-	You want tea, don't you?
ageyou ka?	-	Shall I give you some?
motte kita?	-	Did you bring it?
ookikunatta kara, kirin-san ni natta	-	Now I'm big so I'm a giraffe / I got bigger, so I became a giraffe
nagagutsu de ii?	-	Are boots okay?

---

[25] Literally 'After everyone sleeps, Mummy comes to get me'.

Otousan kuruma ga kuru tte itta	-	Daddy said a car is coming
hayaku itte kite	-	Hurry up and go (and come back)
mata kuru ne	-	We will come back, won't we?
mou yatchatta	-	You've gone and done it now
hantai da yo	-	It's backwards

Day 12

Otousan ga atashi no buranketto yatchatta	-	Daddy did my blanket
gomi ga tsuiteru	-	There is dirt on it
Otousan ga shita ni iru	-	Daddy is downstairs
ima Okaasan terebi miteru	-	Mummy is watching television now
A-chan Pooh-san daisuki	-	A-chan loves Pooh Bear
A-chan kami motteru yo	-	A-chan is holding her hair (up)
dame da yo! gomen nasai wa?	-	That's bad! What about saying sorry?
ugoiteru	-	It's moving[26]
chotto muzukashii	-	It's a bit difficult
shimemasu yo	-	I will close it[27]
omutsu tsukeyou ka?	-	Shall we put the nappy on?
chotto konderu yo	-	It's a bit crowded
abunakunai	-	It's not dangerous
dou yatte kore yaru?	-	How do you do this?
haitchatte	-	In you go / You go in
naosou ka?	-	Shall we fix it?
denwa shiyou ka na?	-	Shall we phone them?
onaka suichatta	-	I'm hungry
Shima-chan owattara iku	-	I'll go when Shima-chan finishes[28]
mottenai yo, okane	-	I don't have any money[29]
kore nani haitteru no?	-	What's inside this?

---

[26] A-chan incorrectly pronounces '*ugoiteru*' (moving) as '*uboiteru*'.
[27] A-chan uses '-*masu*' here because she is acting polite.
[28] Literally 'When Shima-chan finishes I'll go'.
[29] The usual word order would be '*okane mottenai yo*'.

Common mistakes

atarashii aru?	-	Is there a new one?[30]
arukinai	-	I won't walk[31]
nomenai de	-	Don't drink it[32]
kami ga hippatchatta	-	He pulled his hair[33]

Day 13

mou sugu da yo	-	It's very soon
samukunai	-	It's not cold
ja, motte ikou	-	Then, let's take it
naoshite	-	Fix it
te ga tsumetai	-	My hands are cold
T-kun ni aitai naa	-	I'd like to see T-kun[34]
H-kun iru?	-	Will H-kun be there?
ja, kondo ikou nee	-	Then, let's go next time[35]
a! yabai nee	-	Oh! That's a bit risky[36]
seki naotta kara jampu yarou	-	My cough is okay now, so let's do jumping[37]

Day 14

pantsu doko?	-	Where are my underpants?
nai yo	-	They aren't there / They are gone
nakatta yo	-	They weren't there / There were none
kore ribon ga mae	-	The ribbon on this goes at the front
onaka itakatta	-	My stomach hurt (past tense)

---

[30] Should be '*atarashii no ga aru?*' or '*atarashii no aru?*'.
[31] Should be '*arukanai*'.
[32] Should be '*nomanai de*'.
[33] Should be '*kami o hippatchatta*' or just '*kami hippatchatta*'.
[34] Literally 'I want to meet T-kun'.
[35] '*kondo*' means 'this time' or 'next time'.
[36] Although '*yabai*' (dangerous / risky) is slang, it is included here because A-chan used the word.
[37] '*seki naotta*' literally means 'My cough is cured'.

onaka itakunai	-	My stomach doesn't hurt
ottotto...!	-	Oops, oops, oops![38]
konaida mise ikanakatta nee	-	You didn't go to the shop the other day, did you?
obake dete kuru?	-	Will a ghost appear?
A-chan zembu aruita	-	A-chan walked the whole way
A-chan hoikuen hitori de dekita	-	A-chan did nursery school by herself[39]

Day 15

chotto! itai yo, atama	-	Hey! That hurts, my head
mou kurakunai deshou	-	It's not dark anymore, right?
koboshichatta yo, oshikko	-	I spilled them, my wees
Okaasan kenka shichatta yo tte itteru	-	She says Mummy argued
kakurete	-	Hide
mukou ni itchatte	-	Go over there
dame ja nai?	-	That's wrong, isn't it?
kotchi ja nai?	-	Isn't it this way?
gotsun shite atama ga itakatta	-	I bumped it and hurt my head
dou desu ka?	-	How is it?
hajimemashou ka?	-	Shall we start?
ja, hon miyou ka?	-	Then, shall we look at a book?
kagami mite koyou ka?	-	Shall we go and look in the mirror?
hana yada naa	-	Not on my nose / I don't like it on my nose
A-chan aketakatta yo	-	A-chan wanted to open it
beddo no shashin torou	-	Let's take a photo of the bed
dareka kaichatta	-	Somebody has drawn on it

---

[38] Used especially when losing one's balance.
[39] '*dekita*' here means 'was able to do' or 'managed to do'.

Day 16

mukou ni tisshu aru	-	There are tissues over there[40]
A-chan no obentou dekita?	-	Is A-chan's packed lunch ready?
minna suberidai dekiru	-	Everyone can do the slide
mite, kirei ja nai?	-	Look, isn't it pretty?
ikko dake	-	Just one
san-sai ni nattara Otousan yatte ii	-	Daddy can do it when he is three years old
san-sai ni nattara Otousan botan dekiru no	-	Daddy will be able to do his buttons when he is three years old
A-chan ookikunatta kara	-	Because A-chan is big now
konsento yaranai de	-	Don't do the wall socket

Day 17

kore kinai to samukunatchau	-	If you don't wear this you will get cold
wasurechatta	-	I forgot / I have forgotten
kore muzukashii nee	-	This is difficult isn't it
tatanda yo	-	I folded them up
A-chan no tanjoubi Mickey ai ni iku	-	On A-chan's birthday we will go to meet Mickey Mouse
tsukareteru ka naa?	-	I wonder whether she is tired?
tsukaretenai yo	-	She isn't tired
sentaku shiyou	-	Let's wash it / Let's do the washing
doko ni itchatta?	-	Where did it go?
omutsu de shite ii tte itta deshou?	-	You said I can do it in the nappy, right?

Day 18

konnichi wa, hajimemashite	-	Hello, I'm glad to meet you
shuppatsu, ikou!	-	We're off, let's go!
saki kore tabete ii ka na?	-	I wonder whether I can I eat this first?

---

[40] '*tisshu*' is written 'ティシュ'.

shimeru	-	I'll close it
doa shimenai de	-	Don't close the door
pantsu de shichatta	-	I did it in my underpants
te araitai	-	I want to wash my hands
iru? iranai?	-	Do you want some? Or not?
araou ka?	-	Shall we wash them?

Day 19

Otousan, A-chan no asagohan tabenai de kudasai	-	Daddy, please don't eat A-chan's breakfast
oitoite kudasai	-	Please leave it[41]
shawaa shitakatta	-	I wanted to have a shower
A-chan kinou shawaa shita	-	A-chan had a shower yesterday
sagasou ka?	-	Shall we search for it?
sagasou	-	Let's search
san-sai ni narimashita ka?	-	Have you turned three years old?
sugoi hayakatta	-	That was really fast
Okaasan, pantsu de ikou ka?	-	Mummy, shall I go in underpants?
hashitte iku no	-	We will run there

Common mistakes

aketeru	-	It's open[42]

Day 20

koko sawatte ii	-	You can touch here
sawaranai de kudasai	-	Please don't touch it
kore atsui kara	-	Because it's hot
Otousan no karada samui nee	-	Daddy's body is cold, isn't it
ushiro mitai yo	-	I want to look behind it
Okaasan, mienai, terebi!	-	Mummy, I can't see it, the television!

---

[41] '*oitoite*' is a contraction of '*oite oite*', which is from '*oku*' (to put) and '*oku*' (to leave). This can be used to mean 'Put it there and leave it', or just 'Leave it'.

[42] Should be '*aiteru*'.

kyou gohan nani suru?	-	What will we have for dinner today?
hanabi miru hito?	-	Anyone want to watch fireworks?[43]

Day 21

ohayou gozaimasu	-	Good morning
M-chan gakkou itteru	-	M-chan goes to school[44]
takusan oshikko deta yo	-	I did lots of wees / Lots of wees came out
te deteru	-	My hands are sticking out
nani itteru no?	-	What are you saying?
kono ato	-	After this
sekkaku A-chan sentaku shita yo	-	A-chan went to the trouble of washing it
unchi wa muzukashii naa	-	Poos are difficult, aren't they
Okaasan denai yo tte itta no	-	Mummy they won't come out

Day 22

A-chan jibun de tatamu	-	A-chan will fold them up by herself
hai, wakatta!	-	Yes, I understand!
Okaasan yaranai tte itta	-	Mummy said we won't do it
Okaasan ja nai yo, kotchi Okaasan	-	That's not Mummy, this is Mummy here
semai yo	-	It's cramped / It's small / There's no room
mukou ni ikinasai!	-	Go over there!

Common mistakes

nani mo ikanai yo	-	I'm not going anywhere[45]

---

[43] Literally 'People who will watch fireworks?'. This '*-ru hito?*' pattern invites the reply '*hai!*' (Yes!).
[44] '*itteru*' (is going) here is from '*iku*' (to go). It is not '*itteru*' (saying) from '*iu*' (to say).
[45] Should be '*doko ni mo ikanai yo*'.

Day 23

are? minna doushita no?	-	Huh? What happened to everyone?
dame datta?	-	Was it no good? / Didn't it work?
A-chan katazuketa	-	A-chan tidied up / A-chan put them away
hayaku, shawaa shite kite	-	Hurry, go and take a shower
yogorechatta	-	It got all dirty
maa ii yo	-	Well okay then
osampo shimasu	-	I am going for a walk[46]
ii yo tte ittenai	-	She hasn't said it's okay
hitori de dekiru	-	I can do it by myself

Day 24

hatte ii?	-	Can I stick it on?
A-chan takusan unchi deta	-	A-chan did lots of poos
A-chan no dakara tabenai de kudasai	-	It's A-chan's so please don't eat it
kou yatte hippattara...	-	If you pull it like this...
nanika haitchatta	-	Something went inside it

Common mistakes

Otousan, A-chan no futon nenne shinai de	-	Daddy, don't sleep in A-chan's mattress[47]

Day 25

ochichau	-	It will fall down
naichau	-	I'll cry
jibun de yarinasai!	-	Do it by yourself!
A-chan kinou naichatta	-	A-chan cried yesterday
ie ni kaeru yo!	-	I'm going back home!
atashi kore yatteru no	-	I'm doing this

---

[46] Either '*iku*' (go) or '*suru*' (do) can be used with '*sampo*' or '*osampo*' (walk).
[47] Should be '*Otousan, A-chan no futon de nenne shinai de*'.

Okaasan, dou?	- How about you, Mummy?
asobou tte itteru	- He says let's play
te wa makkuro ne	- Your hands are completely black, aren't they
te arawanai to	- We have to wash hands
aka ni natchatta	- It went all red
yubi ga itakatta no	- My finger hurt
shuppatsu shimasu	- We are off now / We will depart
pantsu de oshikko shinai de	- Don't do wees in your underpants

Day 26

Otousan ookikunattara hikouki noru	- Daddy, when you get bigger you can go on an airplane
A-chan ookikunattara nee	- When A-chan gets bigger, okay?
Otousan no koto daisuki	- I love Daddy
futa shimete kudasai	- Please close the lid / Please put the lid on
takushii no naka de tattara dame ne	- You mustn't stand inside the taxi, okay?[48]
zenzen nakatta	- There was nothing there at all
koohii nomanai de	- Don't drink coffee
onegai!	- Please!

Day 27

shitakunai	- I don't want to
taisou shiteru nee	- They are doing exercises, aren't they
shikkari shiteru nee	- He is steady (firm), isn't he
aisatsu shite	- Greet them / Say hello / Say goodbye
ureshii!	- I'm happy! / I'm pleased!
asobitai desu ka?	- Do you want to play?
kyou gohan nan ni shiyou ka?	- What shall we have for dinner today?

---

[48] Remember '*ne*' without '*da*' is feminine speech.

Day 28

konaida koronda kara Otousan otetsudai shite	-	I fell over the other day so please help me Daddy
Otousan mo yatte miyou	-	Daddy, you try it too
ka ni sasarechatta	-	I was bitten by a mosquito / I have a mosquito bite
watashi ga yaritakatta kara	-	Because I wanted to do it
mata yatta	-	I did it again
futari oneesan	-	Two young ladies
teeburu fuiteru	-	I'm wiping the table
hito ga iru kara kotchi haitte mite	-	There are people there so try going in here
jinja de nomu n dakara	-	Because I'll drink it at the shrine
basu kuru ka naa to omotteru nee	-	We are wondering whether the bus will come, aren't we?

Day 29

gomi ni natchatta	-	It is rubbish now[49]
nottara ii ja nai?	-	Wouldn't it be okay to ride?
kanda	-	You bit it
tsume kandara dame deshou nee	-	It's bad to bite your fingernails, right?
okotchau yo, A-chan ga	-	She will get angry, A-chan will
watashi mo nemui	-	I am sleepy too
tatakanai de	-	Don't smack me

Common mistakes

A-chan no zembu dakara sawaranai de kudasai	-	They are all A-chan's so please don't touch them[50]

Day 30

gomi ga nai yo	-	There is no rubbish

---

[49] Literally 'It has become rubbish'.
[50] Should be '*zembu A-chan no dakara...*'.

onigiri to juusu kai ni ikanai to ne	-	We have to go and buy rice-balls and juice
aketara dame deshou	-	We shouldn't open it, right?
mou!	-	Enough! (angry)
toire sawatta kara te arau	-	I touched the toilet so I will wash my hands

Day 31

A-chan no beddo miru dake	-	You can only look at A-chan's bed
watashi ga hippatta	-	I pulled it
semakute...	-	It's cramped, so...
suteki da!	-	It's lovely!
akete miyou	-	Let's open it and see / Let's try to open it
A-chan wa Goofy daisuki ja nai	-	A-chan doesn't love Goofy
ugai shitai	-	I want to rinse my mouth

Two years: Month twelve

Day 1

sugoi deshou?	-	Isn't it amazing? / It's amazing, right?
Jiiji ni agete ii?	-	Can I give it to Grandpa?
asobou to kaite aru	-	It says (written) let's play
kaidan muzukashii	-	Stairs are difficult
onna no ko wa doko?	-	Where is the girl?

Day 2

kore dare yatchatta?	-	Who did this?
genki ni natta	-	I feel better
genki ni nattenai	-	I don't feel better
toritakatta	-	I wanted to fetch it
nenne shitara dame da yo	-	You mustn't sleep
orite kudasai	-	Please get down / Please get off
shinkansen kakkou ii	-	Bullet trains are cool
takusan asonda kara tsukareteru	-	I played a lot so I'm tired / I'm tired because I played a lot
minto kudasai	-	Give me a mint please
ima ofuro hairu?	-	Will you have a bath now?

Day 3

takakatta no?	-	Was it expensive?
A-chan wa oneesan dakara jampu suru	-	A-chan jumps because she is a big girl
A-chan nonjau yo	-	A-chan will drink it
kono ato piza tabete ii?	-	Can I eat pizza after this?[1]
daiji ni shite ne	-	Take care of it / Look after it
daiji ni shinai to	-	You must take care of it / You must look after it
ashi nobashite	-	Stretch out your legs

---

[1] Pizza is most commonly called '*piza*'. A more expensive pizza, say at a restaurant, can be called '*pittsa*'. Another variation, '*pittsua*', is hardly ever used.

Okaasan, onaka itai?	-	Mummy, does your stomach hurt?
chotto muzukashikatta?	-	Was it a bit difficult?

Day 4

dekakeru toki oshikko suru	-	When we (are about to) go out I will do wees
takusan ochitara dame da yo	-	It's bad if lots fall down / Don't let lots fall down
kakkou ii deshou?	-	Isn't that cool?
A-chan kangaruu-san ja nai yo	-	A-chan is not a kangaroo
dekakeru mae ni kiru	-	I will put it on before we go out
tetsudai shiteru no	-	I am helping
kotchi wa watashi no uchi	-	This is my house
A-chan san-sai ni natta kara kore yaru yo	-	A-chan does this because she is three now
hoikuen no tomodachi to onaji	-	It's the same as my friend from nursery school
watashi ga yatta	-	I did it

Common mistakes

toire ni oshikko suru	-	I will do wees in the toilet[2]

Day 5

shusshupoppo	-	Choo choo (train noise)
nuijatta	-	I took it off / I undressed
A-chan ja nai	-	Not A-chan / It wasn't A-chan[3]
ofuro ni hairinasai!	-	Get into the bath! / Take a bath!
ofuro ni hairimasu	-	I will get into the bath
ofuro ni hairanakatta	-	I didn't have a bath
ofuro ni haitteru	-	I am in the bath
ofuro ni hairanai	-	I will not have a bath

---

[2] Should be '*toire de oshikko suru*'.
[3] For example to mean something wasn't her fault.

Notes

> When using 'desu' or '-masu' to sound polite, A-chan pronounces the normally-silent 'u'.

Day 6

ouchi kaetchau	-	I'm going home
e? doushita n darou?	-	Eh? What happened? / I wonder what happened?
A-chan oritai	-	A-chan wants to get off
S-chan no ouchi da yo. M-chan no ouchi wa?	-	That's S-chan's house. What about M-chan's house?
hora, hora, ita! deshou?	-	Look, look, she's there! Right?
kotchi O-chan no uchi da ne	-	Here is O-chan's house
sou shinasai!	-	Do it like that! / You must do it like that!
Okaasan no onaka itakatta	-	Mummy's stomach was hurting
kyoukai ni wasurechatta no	-	We left it at church[4]
tsuite kara minto kudasai	-	Please give me mints after we arrive
shashin tori ni iku no?	-	Are we going to pick up the photos?
chikaramochi da	-	He's a strong man
nemui no	-	I'm sleepy

Common mistakes

tasukete	-	Help me[5]

Day 7

doko iku no?	-	Where are you going?

---

[4] Literally 'We forgot it at church'.
[5] A-chan meant '*tetsudatte*' (assist me), not '*tasukete*' (rescue me).

futtenai n datte	- They say it's not raining[6]
Okaasan katta kara daiji ni shite	- Mummy bought it so take care of it
suberu?	- Will you slide down?
Otousan suberidai daisuki?	- Daddy do you love slides?
mitsukatta	- It was found / They found it
arattenai	- I haven't washed them
onaji deshou?	- They are the same, right?
genki nattenakatta	- I wasn't feeling better
shitteru? shiranai?	- Do you know it? You don't?
Peter Pan doko itchatta no?	- Where did Peter Pan go?
denai n da yo!	- It won't come out!
Otousan tsukutte	- Daddy, make it
kore nuganai de	- Don't take this off (clothes)
iie	- Not at all / Don't mention it[7]
tisshu iru?	- Do you need a tissue?

Day 8

A-chan takusan shiiru yatta	- A-chan did lots of stickers
kono mama de ii?	- Is it okay like this?
Okaasan, doko ni itta?	- Mummy, where did you go?
minna dete kita nee	- They all came out, didn't they?
minto agete ii no?	- Can I give them mints?
ka ni sasareteru	- I have been bitten by a mosquito
kore mitakunai yo	- I don't want to watch this
chuu shinai de	- Don't kiss me
dame datte	- She says no / I'm not allowed
kawaisou tte itteru	- She says she feels sorry for them
kore minasai!	- Look at this! / Watch this! / Look here!
tsume tabeta?	- Did you eat your fingernails?

---

[6] '*datte*' (they say) is more like 'apparently' than '-*te itteru*' (says).
[7] Literally 'No', in reply to being thanked.

Cinderella kudasai	-	Give me Cinderella please
zerii nondenai	-	I haven't been drinking jelly
toire wa itte kita	-	I went to the toilet[8]
osoto wa kurai	-	It is dark outside[9]
gohan tabeyou ka?	-	Shall we have lunch?[10]
machigaeteru yo	-	You have done it wrong
dame dame!	-	No, no! / Don't do that! / That's bad!
hippatteru	-	I am pulling it
osembei kudasai	-	Give me rice crackers please[11]

Day 9

Jiiji motte itchatta no?	-	Did Grandpa take them with him?
mata kowarechatta	-	It broke again
tomattara ne	-	When we stop, alright?
Baaba to Jiiji wa ouchi ni kaetchatta	-	Grandma and Grandpa went back to their house
ashita paatii ikou ka?	-	Shall we go to a party tomorrow?
konaida ochita yo ne	-	They fell down the other day, didn't they?[12]
todokanakatta	-	I couldn't reach them
aratta?	-	Did you wash them?
kigaenasai!	-	Get dressed!
kore kinasai!	-	Wear this! / Put this on!
Otousan, ao to aka dotchi ga ii?	-	Daddy, do you like blue or red?

---

[8] 'wa' here implies a 'but', such as that she went to the toilet but didn't do something else. '*toire ni itte kita*' would mean simply 'I went to the toilet'.

[9] 'wa' here implies outside is dark, as opposed to inside. The distinction is not useful in this case, so it is the same as saying '*osoto ga kurai*' (It is dark outside).

[10] Remember '*gohan*' can be used for any meal.

[11] The honorific 'o' in '*osembei*' is frequently dropped.

[12] '*yo*' emphasizes that it happened, and '*ne*' invites the listener to agree. So '*yo ne*' here is almost like 'didn't they!'.

kore wa yada	-	I don't like this / This is awful
mitsukatta?	-	Was it found?
mitsukaranai	-	It can't be found / We can't find it
mitsukattenai	-	It hasn't been found
ryouhou Okaasan katte kita	-	Mummy went and bought both of them
A-chan koboshita	-	A-chan spilled it
sokkusu wasureteru yo	-	You have forgotten your socks[13]
kono ato onigiri setto ikou ka na?	-	After this shall we go for a rice-balls set meal?
chotto matte, kore tabetara	-	Wait a minute, when I've eaten this
koori ireta?	-	Did you put ice in?
koori irenakatta?	-	You didn't put ice in?
koori iretenai?	-	You haven't put ice in?
nanka yatteru yo nee	-	They're doing something, aren't they[14]

Common mistakes

kore Baaba to Jiiji ageta	-	Grandma and Grandpa gave this to me[15]
chiisai wa taberu?	-	Will you eat the small one?[16]

Day 10

kasa ga tonde itchatta	-	The umbrella flew away
hanasanai de	-	Don't let go
hanashitara dame	-	You mustn't let go
hige yatta?	-	Did you do your beard?
yukkuri tabete kudasai	-	Please eat slowly[17]
waa, ureshii!	-	Oh, I'm so happy!

---

[13] Literally 'You are forgetting your socks'.
[14] *'nanka'* is a contraction of *'nanika'* (something).
[15] Should be *'kore Baaba to Jiiji ga kureta'*.
[16] Should be *'chiisai no wa taberu?'*.
[17] A-chan adds *'kudasai'* here to make the phrase more polite for emphasis.

atarashii pantsu ni shiyou ka?	-	Shall we choose the new underpants?[18]
mae ja nai! ushiro!	-	Not the front! The back!
mukou ni atta no	-	It was over there
e? itta no?	-	Eh? You went?
Otousan minto dame tte itta	-	Daddy said I can't have mints / Daddy said no mints
dashita	-	I spat it out / I put it out
takusan irenai de	-	Don't put lots of them in

Day 11

sawatte	-	Touch it
ii yo, douzo	-	That's fine, go ahead
dekakeru mae ni iku	-	I will go before we go out
akeru? akenai?	-	Will you open it? Or not?
Cinderella mitsuketa!	-	I found Cinderella!
kotchi ni ita	-	She was over here
kore dare ga katte kita no?	-	Who went and bought this?
te ga itakunai no	-	My hand doesn't hurt / My hands don't hurt
mada naiteru	-	I'm still crying
futteru, kyou futteru	-	It's raining, today it's raining

Common mistakes

nurenai to dame dakara motteru yo, kasa	-	We mustn't get wet so I have an umbrella[19]

Day 12

mou ichi-mai aru ka na	-	I wonder whether there is one more?[20]

---

[18] Literally 'Shall we make it the new underpants?'.
[19] Should be '*nuretara dame...*' (musn't get wet), not '*nurenai to dame...*' (must get wet).
[20] '*-mai*' is used for flat objects, like slices of toast and sheets of paper.

A-chan yoru piza tabeta	-	A-chan ate pizza for dinner[21]
nani mo asondenai yo, Okaasan	-	You haven't played with me at all, Mummy
iretoku ne	-	I will put it in, okay?[22]
nani mo kawanai	-	I won't buy anything
nemukunai?	-	Aren't you sleepy?
kaeshite	-	Give it back

Day 13

Otousan, jaketto nuide ne	-	Daddy, take off your jacket
Okaasan ga totte kita	-	Mummy fetched it
minna Happy Birthday utatta	-	Everyone sang Happy Birthday
kyou hoikuen datte	-	She says today is nursery school
mienakunatta yo	-	I can't see it anymore
reizouko ni irete	-	Put it in the fridge

Day 14

kore oitoite ii?	-	Can I leave this here?
Otousan, koohii nominasai!	-	Daddy, drink your coffee!
Okaasan kangaetenai	-	Mummy hasn't decided[23]
gomi yatta?	-	Did you do the rubbish?
DVD nani ga ii?	-	Which DVD would be good?
kusai!	-	It stinks!
kowakunakatta	-	I wasn't scared
Otousan no wa?	-	What about Daddy's?
paatii A-chan no uchi de yatta	-	We had the party at A-chan's home

Day 15

kore dake	-	Just this / Only these
chiisaku yatte yo, chiisaku	-	Make it small, small

---

[21] Literally 'A-chan ate pizza in the evening'.
[22] '*iretoku*' is a contraction of '*irete oku*' (to put in and leave it).
[23] Literally 'Mummy hasn't thought about it'.

oishikunai desu	-	It doesn't taste good
kitchin de	-	In the kitchen
Okaasan to onaji	-	It's the same as Mummy / Mummy's is the same
koboshitenai yo	-	I haven't spilt it
kore wa yogoreteru	-	This is dirty
chotto dake asonde te ne	-	Play just a little bit, will you?
chotto dake asobou ka?	-	Shall we play just a little bit?

Day 16

hayaku mitai	-	I want to see it soon[24]
ikinasai, anta!	-	You, go![25]
A-chan naoshite ii?	-	May A-chan fix it?
nakatta?	-	It wasn't there? / Weren't there any?
nani kau no?	-	What will you buy?
minna arigatou!	-	Thank you everyone!
Otousan ga kotchi haittara dame da	-	Daddy is not allowed to go in here
mata asobou ne	-	Let's play again (some time)
Pocahontas no DVD mitai yo	-	I want to watch the Pocahontas DVD
Pooh-san mo mitai naa	-	I'd like to watch Pooh Bear too[26]
ashita ame da ne	-	It will rain tomorrow, won't it?[27]
yarou ka?	-	Shall we do it?
Otousan chiisakunattara hairu	-	Daddy will be able to fit in when he gets smaller
Okaasan sekkaku sentaku shita kara dame	-	You mustn't because Mummy went to the trouble of washing them

---

[24] Literally 'I want to see it quickly'.
[25] '*anta*' is a contraction of '*anata*' (you) that is very casual and can sound either intimate or derogatory.
[26] Depending on the context this could also mean 'Pooh Bear wants to watch too'.
[27] Literally 'Tomorrow is rain, isn't it?'.

Day 17

M-chan to I-san to tsukutta	-	I made it with M-chan and I-san
otomodachi to te tsunaida	-	I held hands with a friend[28]
fukuro irimasu ka?	-	Do you need a bag?[29]
omokute yada	-	I don't like it this heavy[30]
A-chan wa tsukaretenai	-	A-chan is not tired
minna kotchi ni hairu?	-	Will everyone go in here? / Can everyone fit in here?
itte kimasu	-	Off I go
ireyou ka?	-	Shall I put some in? / Shall I put it in?

Day 18

asa nattara Baaba to Jiiji iru yo	-	Grandma and Grandpa will be here in the morning[31]
asa nattara nenne shitara dame da	-	You mustn't sleep in the morning[32]
nemutai?	-	Are you sleepy?
kondo itte ne	-	Go next time
mou ii yo!	-	That's enough! / I'm ready!
te wa kirei da yo	-	My hands are clean

Day 19

hayaku kaeru?	-	Will you come home early?
Okaasan, omiyage!	-	Mummy, a present![33]
oite aru?	-	Was it left there? / Has it been left there?

---

[28] The 'o' in 'otomodachi' is honorific, and can sound childish in casual speech.
[29] A-chan used the polite '-*masu*' form here because she was pretending to be a shop assistant.
[30] Literally 'It's heavy and horrible'.
[31] The particle '*ni*' is implied: '*asa nattara...*' (when it becomes morning).
[32] '-*tara*' is used twice here, in '*nattara*' (when it becomes) to mean 'when', and in '*shitara*' (if you do) to mean 'if'.
[33] '*omiyage*' also means 'souvenir'.

mawarou yo	-	Let's go round and round
ashita hayaku NanDeemo iku	-	We will go to Nandeemo early tomorrow
kotchi ni irenai de	-	Don't put them in here
ima tsukutteru	-	I'm making it now
shikkari shinasai!	-	Watch what you're doing! / Steady on![34]

Day 20

saki Okaasan oshikko shite kudasai	-	Mummy please do wees first
ikitakatta	-	I wanted to go
shiroi pantsu ga ii	-	I want the white underpants
hairenai	-	It won't go in / I can't get in
kore A-chan no jaketto to Otousan no pantsu	-	This is A-chan's jacket and Daddy's underpants
ja, tatte yarou ka?	-	Then, shall we do it standing up?
todoku yo!	-	It reaches! / I can reach!
owattenakatta?	-	Wasn't it finished?

Day 21

kirei desu	-	It's pretty / It's clean
shimatteru	-	They are closed / It's closed (shop)
akeyou?	-	Shall we open it?
kore shimatte	-	Put these away
A-chan ga yaritakatta	-	A-chan wanted to do it
kore de?	-	In this? / In these? / With this?
Otousan wa byouki ja nai	-	Daddy is not sick
A-chan wa byouin iku	-	A-chan will go to the hospital

---

[34] '*shikkari shinasai*' can also mean 'Pull yourself together' or 'Don't give up'.

Common mistakes

kore Okaasan no zembu da yo	-	These are all Mummy's[35]
aisukuriimu jinja ni tabeyou yo	-	Let's eat ice-cream at the shrine[36]

Day 22

okinai to nee	-	We'll have to get up, won't we
netsu hakaru	-	I will take my temperature
A-chan ouma-san kowakunai wa	-	A-chan is not afraid of horses[37]
ouji-sama ga dete kara	-	After the prince appears
sawattenai	-	I haven't touched it
Otousan mo katazukeru yo	-	Daddy will clear up too
kore na no	-	It's this one[38]
anmitsu na no?	-	Is it bean jam in syrup?[39]
kore minna no na no?	-	Is this everyone's, is that it?[40]
hantai no sokkusu nakatta yo	-	The opposite sock wasn't there
Otousan, isshoni miyou	-	Daddy, let's watch it together
asa ni natta no ne	-	Well, it's morning
tsumetai ocha kudasai	-	Please give me cold tea
tabecha dame	-	Don't eat it / You mustn't eat it[41]

Day 23

A-chan wa doko ni iku no?	-	Where will A-chan go?
Okaasan wa tatte dekinai	-	Mummy can't do it standing up

---

[35] Should be '*kore zembu Okaasan no da yo*'.
[36] Should be '*aisukuriimu jinja de tabeyou yo*'.
[37] The trailing '*wa*' is feminine speech, and is written as 'わ'. The meaning is similar to '*yo*', but softer. The particle 'は' is also spelt as '*wa*' in this book, but is written as '*ha*' in some variants of Romaji.
[38] When used at the end of a statement, '*na no*' is like '*desu*' (is), and is feminine speech.
[39] When used as a question, '*na no?*' is like '*desu ka?*' (is it?), and can be used by anyone.
[40] The construction here is '*minna no*' (everyone's) plus '*na no?*' (is it?).
[41] '*tabecha*' is a contraction of '*tabete wa*'.

A-chan wa miruku ga suki	-	A-chan likes milk
koko ni ishi ga haitchatta	-	A stone got in here
taihen da yo!	-	Oh no! / That's terrible![42]
kowarechau yo!	-	It will break!
ikitakunai	-	I don't want to go
ittenai	-	She didn't say / She hasn't said[43]
kore motte tabete oishii no	-	It tastes good to hold this and eat it
kusakunai	-	It doesn't stink

Notes

> A-chan is starting to include particles to make her sentences a little longer, but only when she is confident of which ones to use.

Day 24

kawaikatta	-	It was cute
nani hajimaru no?	-	What will start?
mou ichi-mai wa?	-	What about another slice?
kotchi ga konderu	-	It's crowded here
sugoi konderu nee	-	It's really crowded, isn't it
kore motte aruite	-	Hold this and walk
kore ni suru?	-	Will you have this one?
katte ikitai	-	I want to buy it before we go[44]
futteru nee	-	It's raining, isn't it
A-chan boushi kabutteru	-	A-chan is wearing a hat
Otousan A-chan oshichatta	-	Daddy pushed A-chan
isshoni ikou tte itta	-	She said let's go together
isshoni ikou datte	-	She says let's go together
denai no?	-	It won't come out?

---

[42] Previously A-chan had said only '*taihen!*'.
[43] This phrase could also mean 'She hasn't gone'.
[44] Literally 'I want to buy it and go'.

Day 25

A-chan takusan nonjau wa	-	A-chan will drink a lot / A-chan drinks a lot
Cinderella kaite miyou	-	Let's try to draw Cinderella
Cinderella no kutsu kaite	-	Draw Cinderella's shoes
ouji-sama no zubon kaite ne	-	Draw the Prince's trousers
shite minai?	-	Won't you try it?
naku yo	-	I will cry
A-chan ga naku	-	A-chan will cry
Okaasan onaka ga samui kara tsukete te tte itta no	-	Mummy said put it on because her tummy is cold[45]

Common mistakes

Disneyland no Pinocchio ni itta	-	We went to see Pinocchio at Disneyland[46]

Day 26

hayaku ikanai to	-	You must go quickly
hayaku kaette kita?	-	Did you come home early?
shigoto ni itta?	-	Did you go to work?
kou yatte motte te, kotchi oite mite	-	Hold it like this, and try putting it over here
kou shite	-	Do it like this
ouchi de gohan tabeta	-	We ate dinner at home
sekkaku Baaba ga katte kita kara daiji ni shite ne	-	Grandma bought it specially, so take care of it
aru deshou?	-	They are there, right?
motte kaette ii yo	-	You can take it home
takushii de itte ne	-	Go by taxi
zembu A-chan no kaado	-	They are all A-chan's cards

---

[45] The construction here is '*tsukete te*' (put it on) plus '*tte itta*' (she said).
[46] Should be '*Disneyland ni Pinocchio ai ni itta*'.

Common mistakes

A-chan to Okaasan hoikuen ni tsukutta	-	A-chan and Mummy made it at nursery school[47]

Day 27

Minnie-chan mienakunatchatta	-	I can't see Minnie Mouse anymore
O-chan hagu daisuku datte	-	She says O-chan loves hugs
futari yatte ii yo	-	The two of you can do it
kimono wa nagai yo ne	-	The kimono is long, isn't it
suwarinasai!	-	Sit down!
minasan, tabete kudasai	-	Everyone, please eat
minasan itadakimasu	-	Everyone, we will now eat

Common mistakes

koko atakunai	-	It is not warm here[48]

Day 28

Maria-chan to Rika-chan oite kichatta	-	I left Maria and Licca-chan (dolls) behind
kyou hoikuen desu yo	-	Today is nursery school
pajama ni tsuiteru	-	It's (stuck) on my pajamas
yada, itai yo!	-	No, it hurts!
yatte mitai	-	I want to try it
Otousan, irimasu ka?	-	Daddy, do you want some?
J-kun, A-chan to asobitai tte itta	-	J-kun said he wants to play with A-chan
S-chan mo itta	-	S-chan said it too
tsumetakunai yo	-	It doesn't feel cold

Day 29

sannin de, A-chan to Okaasan to Otousan	-	The three of us, A-chan, Mummy and Daddy

---

[47] Should be '… *hoikuen de tsukutta*'.
[48] Should be '*atatakakunai*' or '*attakakunai*'.

Otousan wa oniku ga ii	- Daddy wants meat / Daddy likes meat
Otousan wa oniku ga daisuku	- Daddy loves meat
saki itte ii?	- Can I go on ahead?
Otousan yasashii nee	- Daddy is kind, isn't he
Okaasan yasashikunai	- Mummy is not kind
Otousan mo Okaasan mo yasashii	- Daddy and Mummy are both kind
gacha gacha gurutto mawashitai	- I want to turn the (knob on the) gacha gacha machine
Otousan, toire ikinasai!	- Daddy, go to the toilet!
kesanai de	- Don't turn it off
A-chan sugoi tsukarechatta	- A-chan is really tired
sugoi A-chan tsukarechatta	- A-chan is really tired
Peter Pan mitara nenne suru	- I will sleep after watching Peter Pan[49]
otsuki-sama nai nee	- There is no moon[50]
aka ni natteru	- They have gone red[51]
zembu tabechatta yo ne!	- You ate everything, didn't you!
kore mou chotto yatte	- Do this a bit more
futari hayakatta nee	- You were both quick, weren't you
aru aru!	- There are some!

Common mistakes

Otousan kuruma de hairenakatta	- Daddy couldn't get in because of the car[52]

Day 30

Okaasan ouchi ni iru yo	- Mummy is at home
sawatte, sawatte mite	- Touch it, try touching it
ouchi de shiyou ne	- Let's do it at home

---

[49] Literally 'I will sleep when I watch Peter Pan'.
[50] '*otsuki-sama*' is a children's word for '*tsuki*' (moon).
[51] A-chan said this at traffic lights. She used '*natteru*' (have become) instead of '*natta*' (became) because the lights were still red.
[52] Should be '*Otousan kuruma ga atta kara hairenakatta*'.

ippai happa torechatta ne	-	Lots of leaves have come off
neko-chan ugoiteta yo	-	The pussy cat was moving
Otousan mo surippa haite	-	Daddy, you put your slippers on too
ongaku owatchau	-	The music will finish / The music is going to finish
obake ga konai yo	-	Ghosts won't come / There won't be any ghosts
ocha itte ii yo	-	You can go and have tea[53]

Common mistakes

A-chan tonari	-	Next to A-chan[54]

---

[53] *'ocha'* (tea) is special in that it is commonly used to mean 'drink tea'. So you can say *'ocha iku'* (I will go to have tea) or *'ocha shiyou'* (Let's have tea). For other drinks you would have to say, for example, *'koohii nomi ni iku'* (I will go and drink coffee) or *'koohii nomou'* (Let's drink coffee).

[54] Should be *'A-chan no tonari'*.

Three years: Month one

"*san-sai*" – Three years old

Day 1

A-chan hitori de suru	-	A-chan will do it by herself
O-chan onaji jaketto	-	O-chan has the same jacket
O-chan kutsu onaji deshou?	-	O-chan has the same shoes, right?
Otousan shigoto ikanai to	-	Daddy has to go to work
hoikuen ikitai naa	-	I'd like to go to nursery school
kotchi hoikuen na no	-	This way is nursery school
Okaasan ga koronda	-	Mummy fell over
Okaasan ga koronjatta	-	Mummy fell over
sou da yo!	-	That's right!
itte kimashita	-	We went (and came back) / We went there

Common mistakes

Otousan to ofuro de haitta	-	I had a bath with Daddy[1]

Day 2

Okaasan koronda kara byouin iku	-	Mummy fell over, so we will go to the hospital
Otousan korondara bandoeido petanko shiyou yo	-	If Daddy falls over, let's stick a Band-Aid on him[2]
Otousan mo chi ga detara petanko suru	-	If Daddy bleeds, we will stick one on him too
miteru dake	-	Just looking
demo byouki ja nai yo	-	But I'm not sick

---

[1] Should be '*Otousan to ofuro ni haitta*'.
[2] '*bandoeido haru*' would sound less childish.

Otousan totte kite	-	Daddy, go and get it
Okaasan waratteru	-	Mummy is laughing
Okaasan warattenai	-	Mummy is not laughing
te tsunaide	-	Hold hands
Otousan no te mo tsumetai ne	-	Daddy's hands are cold too
kore ga dame	-	This is no good
oyatsu tabetai	-	I want to eat snacks
chotto dake aruita yo	-	I walked just a little bit

Day 3

iro ga aru	-	It is coloured / It has colour
tanoshii yo!	-	It's fun!
ryouhou wa dame	-	You can't have them both[3]
mou chotto aruku	-	I will walk a little bit more
motte kaetta	-	I brought it home
Zenmai hajimatchau	-	Zenmai Zamurai is going to start (on TV)
kurakunattara nenne suru	-	I will sleep when it gets dark
Okaasan neko-chan mitai da ne	-	Mummy is like a pussy cat
Otousan nan ni mieru?	-	What does Daddy look like?
zembu ja nai	-	Not all of them
hairanai desu	-	It won't go in / It doesn't fit
doonatsu-ya-san	-	A donut shop[4]

Day 4

O-chan Rika-chan motteru	-	O-chan has a Licca-chan doll

---

[3] '*wa*' here emphasizes '*ryouhou*' (both), so '*ryouhou wa dame*' means 'You can't have both'. Without '*wa*', '*ryouhou dame*' would mean 'You can't have either of them', literally 'Both are bad'.
[4] The '-*ya*' or '-*ya-san*' suffix can be used for other shops too, such as '*pan-ya*' or '*pan-ya-san*' (bakery), and '*sushi-ya*' or '*osushi-ya-san*' (sushi shop).

kore kara hajimaru yo	-	It will start after this / It will start now[5]
Okaasan akachan haitteru	-	Mummy has a baby inside[6]
Okaasan to Otousan to A-chan koko de nenne suru	-	Mummy and Daddy and A-chan will sleep here
obake konai?	-	Ghosts won't come?
A-chan no onigiri tsukutte kudasai tte itta, Okaasan ni kazoeteru	-	I said please make A-chan's rice-balls, to Mummy
	-	I am counting
Otousan, asonde ii desu yo	-	Daddy, you can play
itterasshai	-	See you later / Have a good day[7]
summahen	-	Excuse me[8]

Day 5

Okaasan to haitta	-	I went in with Mummy
haittara dame	-	You mustn't go in
konaida Goofy dete kita deshou?	-	Goofy was on (television) the other day, right?
kore yamete kudasai	-	Please stop doing this
kaado wasureta n desu ne	-	You forgot the card, didn't you
daijoubu desu ne	-	It's okay, isn't it
kore wa ikura desu ka?	-	How much does this cost?
dekinai no?	-	Can't you do it?

Day 6

Otousan wa tonari ni nenne shite ne	-	Daddy, sleep next to me
A-chan onaka ookikunatchatta	-	A-chan's stomach has become bigger
Otousan no megane wa onaji da ne	-	Daddy's glasses are the same, aren't they

---

[5] '*kore kara*' literally means 'after this', but can also mean 'now'.
[6] Like the English, this sounds childish.
[7] '*itterasshai*' (See you later) is the standard response to '*itte kimasu*' (I'm off).
[8] '*summahen*' is Kyoto dialect for '*sumimasen*' (excuse me). A-chan picked this up from a television drama.

ippai atta	-	There were lots of them
A-chan to kaite aru	-	It says "A-chan" (written)
Okaasan ga kaita	-	Mummy wrote it
Otousan suwatteru	-	Daddy is sitting
kore omiyage	-	This is a present / This is a souvenir
nagai desu yo	-	It's so long
sukunakunatteru	-	There are fewer of them[9]

Common mistakes

tsumetai yarou ka?	-	Shall we make it cold?[10]
Otousan no ue de basu noru?	-	Will the (toy) bus go over Daddy?[11]

Day 7

Otousan funderu	-	Daddy is standing on it
shitagi nuretenai, oshikko de	-	The underwear is not wet, with wees
nani sore?	-	What's that?
nan darou ne	-	What could it be
owattara kore kiyou	-	When it finishes let's wear this / Let's put this on when it finishes
iranai desu ne	-	You don't want it, do you
kore ga Kitty-chan tsuitenai	-	This doesn't have Hello Kitty on it[12]
osara motte tabete ne	-	Hold the plate and eat / Eat it holding the plate
hayaku nonjatta	-	You drank it quickly
onaji ga ii no	-	I want one the same[13]
watashi ni kawatte	-	Pass the (phone) call to me
ijiwaru shinai de	-	Don't be mean

---

[9] Literally 'They have become fewer', from '*sukunai*' (few).
[10] Should be '*tsumetaku yarou ka?*'.
[11] Should be '*Otousan no ue ni basu iku?*'.
[12] '*tsuitenai*' (not attached) here is from '*tsuku*' (to be attached), not '*tsuku*' (to arrive).
[13] '*onaji no ga ii no*' is more technically correct, but '*onaji ga ii no*' is acceptable in speech.

Day 8

kore watashi no da yo	-	This is mine
sou da yo ne	-	That's right, isn't it
minna, sagashite miyou ka?	-	Everyone, shall we try looking for it?
doko ka naa?	-	I wonder where it is?
ii desu ne, hai!	-	That's good, okay!
Otousan daijoubu da yo	-	Daddy is alright
sakki nakatta	-	It wasn't there before
maa ii ya	-	Oh well[14]

Day 9

Otousan ni tsukeyou	-	Let's put it on Daddy
hoikuen no kaban ga nai yo	-	My nursery school bag is not here
dare mo inakatta	-	Nobody was there[15]
kotchi samukunai	-	It's not cold over here
Tigger mo ita	-	Tigger was there too
kotchi de tabete ii?	-	Can I eat over here?
oneesan chotto matte te tte itta nee	-	The young lady said to wait a minute, didn't she

Day 10

kyou keeki tori ni iku	-	We will collect the cake today
Otousan mo ikou yo	-	Daddy, you go too
ii yo, daijoubu	-	It's okay, it's alright
A-chan onaka suita kara asagohan kudasai	-	A-chan is hungry so give me breakfast please
mada unchi tsuiteru	-	It still has poo on it
konaida chiisai unchi ga dekita yo	-	The other day I did a small poo

---

[14] '*ii ya*' means 'No' when used by itself or at the start of a phrase. Otherwise it means 'Oh well' or 'It will do', as in '*sore de ii ya*' (That will do).
[15] Literally 'There wasn't anyone'.

Day 11

Tinkerbell dotchi ga ii ka na tte itteru	-	Tinkerbell is saying, I wonder which is better?
shitagi kite ii n datte	-	She says I can wear underwear
kakurete tabeteru	-	I am hiding and eating / I'm eating secretly
kyou takusan miruku nonde ii desu ka?	-	May I drink lots of milk today?
minai de kudasai	-	Please don't look
mienakunatchatta	-	I can't see it anymore

Day 12

T-shatsu ni suru?	-	Shall we make it the T-shirt?
ima T-shatsu ga nai yo	-	There isn't a T-shirt now
akakunatchatta	-	It went red
umareta	-	She was born
Otousan ga motte, A-chan ga shashin toru	-	Daddy, you hold it and A-chan will take the photo

Day 13

kami ga nagai nee	-	Your hair is long, isn't it
ii ja nai?	-	Isn't that okay?
Kitty-chan Jingle Bells utatta	-	Hello Kitty sang Jingle Bells
A-chan taberenai	-	A-chan can't eat it[16]
Otousan ga kitta	-	Daddy cut it
ato, I-chan wa?	-	And, what about I-chan?
Otousan ga funda	-	Daddy stood on it
koko ni hairanai de	-	Don't come in here
Otousan mo da yo!	-	Daddy too!
ofuro ni hairitakunai	-	I don't want to get in the bath / I don't want to have a bath

---

[16] '*taberenai*' is a contraction of '*taberarenai*' (can't eat).

Day 14

te dashite	-	Hold out your hand / Put your hand out
mazukatta?	-	Did it taste bad?
dareka katazuketa	-	Someone cleaned up
nan dakke?	-	What was it again?[17]
konaida Disneyland ni I-chan to M-chan to itta	-	We went to Disneyland the other day with I-chan and M-chan
koko ni ireta n desu	-	I put it in here

Common mistakes

happa motchatta	-	I picked up a leaf[18]
dekirenai	-	I can't do it[19]
dekireru?	-	Can you do it?[20]

Day 15

konaida NanDeemo ni itta n desu yo	-	We went to Nandeemo the other day[21]
koko de baibai suru	-	We will say bye bye here
A-chan pan tabeteru	-	A-chan is eating bread
A-chan hitori de gambatteru	-	A-chan is doing her best by herself
gomen ja nai!	-	Not 'sorry'! / Don't just say 'sorry'!
Goofy, doko ni haitteru?	-	Goofy, where are you? / Goofy, what are you inside?

Day 16

naite ii yo	-	You can cry / It's okay to cry
Minnie-chan ga mae	-	Minnie Mouse goes at the front
chanto doresu kinasai!	-	Put your dress on properly!
mata kiyou yo	-	Let's wear it again (sometime)

---

[17] '*dakke*' is used when trying to recall something.
[18] Should be '*happa hirotta*'.
[19] Should be '*dekinai*'.
[20] Should be '*dekiru?*'.
[21] '*-n desu yo*' is very polite.

Otousan utatchatta	-	Daddy sang[22]

Day 17

hana deteru	-	Your nose is running
ato wa nai	-	There aren't any more / There are no more
kitchin de yaru	-	I will do it in the kitchen
ima kore yatteru	-	I am doing this now
baikin ga tsuiteru	-	There are germs on it

Common mistakes

dore ni taoru suru?	-	Which towel shall we use?[23]

Day 18

koko ni oite okou ne	-	Let's leave it here, shall we?
kore wa motteru n da	-	I'm holding this
hayaku motte kite	-	Bring it quickly
kyou S-chan inakatta	-	S-chan wasn't there today
J-kun wa ita	-	J-kun was there
oyatsu nai yo	-	There are no snacks
jumban da yo	-	We take turns[24]

Day 19

futatsu aru	-	There are two
S-chan wakannai	-	S-chan doesn't know
motte konakatta n deshou?	-	You didn't bring it, right?
mou ikkai dete kuru	-	He will appear once more
Minnie-chan Cinderella miteta n da	-	Minnie Mouse was watching Cinderella

---

[22] '*-chatta*' here implies it wasn't supposed to happen.
[23] Should be '*dono taoru tsukau?*'.
[24] '*jumban*' is written in hiragana with an '*n*' (ん), but spelt in Romaji here as '*m*' since this is how it is pronounced. Other common words like this are '*gambaru*' (to do your best) and '*shimbun*' (newspaper).

Otousan pan katte kite tte itta n deshou?	-	She told Daddy to go and buy bread, right?[25]
Disneyland ni Ariel ga dete kuru	-	Ariel appears at Disneyland

Day 20

mou nai yo	-	There aren't any more / There are none left
chotto, koborechau kara yukkuri tabete	-	Hey, eat slowly or it will spill[26]
atarashii no atta	-	I found a new one / I found the new one
Otousan wa pajama kiteru yo	-	Daddy is wearing pajamas
kore haato no aka	-	This is a red heart
kowakatta?	-	Were you scared?
motto kowakatta?	-	Were you more scared?
hitori de ikanai de	-	Don't go by yourself
A-chan arukitai	-	A-chan wants to walk
tsunagou yo	-	Let's hold (hands)
koko ni irete kudasai	-	Please put it in here
A-chan peropero shiteru	-	A-chan is licking it

Common mistakes

kore dou yatte yaru wakaranai	-	I don't know how to do this[27]
atarashii tsukaitai	-	I want to use the new one[28]
Otousan mo omoi	-	It's heavy for Daddy too[29]

Day 21

A-chan onara shita	-	A-chan broke wind

---

[25] The particle '*ni*' is implied: '*Otousan ni...*'. If the implied particle had been '*wa*', the meaning would become 'Daddy said to go and buy bread, right?'.
[26] Literally 'Hey, it will spill so eat slowly'.
[27] Should be '*kore dou yatte yaru ka wakaranai*'.
[28] Should be '*atarashii no tsukaitai*'.
[29] Should be '*Otousan ni mo omoi*'.

gomi sutete kite	-	Go and throw out the rubbish
kigaemasu ne	-	I'll change clothes, alright
nanka kikoeta	-	I heard something
hana fuita, tisshu de	-	I wiped my nose, with a tissue
kao aratte massaaji shiteru	-	She is washing and massaging her face
kowarechatta kara naoshiteru no	-	It broke so I'm fixing it
ii ko ni shiteru kara obake wa konai	-	I am being good, so ghosts won't come
Okaasan kaette kite arigatou ne	-	Mummy, thanks for coming home
hai, hoikuen itteru n desu	-	Yes, I attend nursery school

Day 22

hayaku nonjau yo	-	I will drink it quickly
kurakunattara kite ne	-	Come when it gets dark, alright?
shou ga nai	-	Never mind / It can't be helped
kampai shiyou ka?	-	Shall we make a toast?
kawaisou da yo ne!	-	You poor thing!
arere?	-	Huh?[30]
kore wa dore ni suru?	-	Which one of these do you want?
kore wa dore ni shimasu ka?	-	Which one of these do you want?
kore wa mita n desu ne	-	We saw this one, didn't we
kore wa chotto nagai desu ne	-	This is a little bit long, isn't it
nagakunai desu ne	-	It isn't long, is it
kabocha no suupu nonde, gohan tabemashita	-	I drank pumpkin soup, and ate rice
pinku ni shite ii?	-	Can I have the pink one?
A-chan Maki-chan motte nenne suru	-	A-chan will take Maki-chan (doll) to sleep
chotte matte!	-	Wait a minute!

---

[30] A longer form of '*are?*' (huh?).

jaketto kitenai ja nai?	- You are not wearing your jacket, are you?[31]

Day 23

Otousan no kaisha no paatii, Santa-san ga kita	- Santa came to Daddy's company party
atode yarou yo	- Let's do it later
Otousan no motte kimasu	- I will bring Daddy's
A-chan wa aka ni suru	- A-chan will have the red one
kiiro no maru	- Yellow circle
okao mite	- Look at my face
ashi ga itai	- My leg hurts
samukunai ja nai	- It's not cold, is it
Okaasan ga oshieta no	- Mummy told me / Mummy taught me
onaka ippai yo	- I am full / My stomach is full
tabe ni itta	- We went to eat
watashi ga notteta	- I was riding on it

Day 24

atari!	- Correct!
tabetara dame da yo	- You must not eat it
tsumetakunatchatta	- It got cold
a, tsukatteru n desu ka?	- Oh, are you using it?
ue ni, ue ni!	- Up, up!
ue ni iku kara	- Because it will go up
kore kitchin ni atta no	- This was in the kitchen

Day 25

minna tatte kudasai	- Everyone please stand up
kawaii doresu kite ii?	- Can I wear the cute dress?
konaida A-chan ga nenne	- Santa came the other day when

---

[31] This question is a double negative, literally 'Aren't you not wearing your jacket?'.

shitara Santa-san ga kita	-	A-chan went to sleep
Santa-san ouchi ni kaetchatta, Okaasan ga itteru	-	Mummy says Santa has gone home
tonakai-san desu	-	It's a reindeer
arigato ne	-	Thanks
Otousan mo kite ne	-	Daddy you come too okay?
fuite ageru	-	I'll wipe it for you
doko ni itchatta ka na?	-	I wonder where it went?
ashita byouin ni iku	-	We will go to the hospital tomorrow
Okaasan seki ga deta kara	-	Because Mummy has a cough
funyafunya shiteru	-	It's limp / It's squishy[32]

Common mistakes

tattetenakatta deshou	-	You weren't standing up[33]

Day 26

A-chan byouin ni itte chuusha shita no	-	A-chan went to the hospital and had an injection
sensei ni moratta	-	I got it from the doctor / The doctor gave it to me
kagi torenakatta	-	I couldn't reach the key
hamigaki yatte ii?	-	Can I brush my teeth?
wanchan unchi shichatta	-	The dog did a poo
unchi ga tsuiteru	-	It has poo on it
Okaasan, tadaima!	-	Mummy, I'm home!

"*tadaima*" – We're home!

---

[32] '*funyafunya*' is spelt '*fu-nya-fu-nya*' (ふにゃふにゃ), not '*fun-ya-fun-ya*' (ふんやふんや).
[33] Should be '*tattenakatta deshou*'.

Day 27

onaka ga itai kara dakko shite	-	My stomach hurts so carry me
Cinderella pinku doresu da yo	-	Cinderella has the pink dress
Peter Pan to warui hito	-	Peter Pan and the bad person
sugoi desu ne	-	It's amazing, isn't it
ja, mou ikkai haitte kudasai	-	Then, please go in once more
dekinakunatchatta	-	I can't do it anymore
Otousan tsume tabenai de	-	Daddy, don't eat your nails
konaida Okaasan doko ni itchatta n dakke?	-	Where did Mummy go the other day again?
minna kusuri nonderu	-	Everyone is drinking medicine[34]
kami ga ochiru	-	Your hair is falling down
toorenai	-	I can't get through / I can't pass by

Day 28

netsu ga aru kara ikanai	-	I have a fever so I won't go
dou shiyou nee?	-	What shall we do?
Otousan atode tabete ii	-	Daddy you can eat it later
tsumetakatta	-	It was cold / It felt cold
Otousan ga oroshita	-	Daddy got it down
Baaba to Jiiji hikouki de kaetchatta	-	Grandma and Grandpa went back by airplane
Otousan kawaii kara shashin toritai naa	-	Daddy is so cute I'd like to take his photo
Otousan no jaketto ni nenne shitakatta	-	I wanted to sleep in Daddy's jacket
konaida Otousan no kaisha no paatii ni, Kitty-chan Jingle Bells utatta	-	At Daddy's company party recently, Hello Kitty sang Jingle Bells

Day 29

kore bazaa de katte kita no	-	We bought this at the bazaar
nani mo minai yo	-	I won't watch anything

---

[34] A-chan incorrectly pronounces '*kusuri*' (medicine) as '*sukuri*'.

Okaasan kaechatte	-	Mummy (please) change it
kobosanakatta	-	I didn't spill it
kangaete	-	Think about it
gomi sutete kita?	-	Did you go and throw the rubbish away?

Common mistakes

okawari shite	-	Another helping please[35]
kao ni tsukechatta	-	I got it on my face[36]
Santa-san ni ageta	-	Santa gave it to me[37]

Day 30

memo shinai de!	-	Don't take notes!
kore aketai	-	I want to open this
kyou nai desu	-	There are none today
kikoenai	-	I can't hear it
aa omoshiroi	-	Oh, that's funny
akeyou ka?	-	Shall we open it?
Otousan to tabeyou	-	Let's eat with Daddy

Day 31

osoi nee!	-	You're late, aren't you!
hayaku kaette kite	-	Hurry up and come home / Come home early
Okaasan osokatta	-	Mummy was late
Otousan ga yatte	-	Daddy, you do it
chotto abunai yo	-	It's a bit dangerous
oshouyu tsuketai	-	I want to put soy sauce on it[38]

---

[35] Should be '*okawari kudasai*' (Another helping please), since '*okawari shite*' would mean 'Have another helping'.
[36] Should be '*kao ni tsuichatta*' (I got it on my face), since '*kao ni tsukechatta*' would mean 'I put it on my face'.
[37] Should be '*Santa-san ga kureta*'.
[38] The '*o*' in '*oshouyu*' (soy sauce) is honorific.

koko ni iretai	-	I want to put it in here
dareka ochichatta?	-	Did someone fall off?

Three years: Month two

Day 1

Otousan oshigoto ni ikanai deshou?	-	Daddy, you're not going to work, right?
Okaasan okoru	-	Mummy will get angry
baggu funderu	-	You're standing on my bag
minna samui desu ka?	-	Is everyone cold?
Otousan soto de Jingle Bells yatte kudasai	-	Daddy, please do Jingle Bells outside
haitte kite	-	Come in
namae nan dakke?	-	What's his name again?
Jiiji no kuruma de ikou yo	-	Let's go in Grandpa's car

Common mistakes

Okaasan sagashita	-	Mummy found it[1]
Baaba to Jiiji de te arawanakatta	-	I didn't wash my hands with Grandma and Grandpa[2]

Day 2

youfuku kangaete	-	Think about clothes / Think about what I will wear
dare ga haitteru ka naa?	-	I wonder who is inside?
otomodachi motte kaetchatta?	-	Did another child take it away?[3]
ouchi ni kaeritai	-	I want to go back home
ippai shimatteru	-	Many (of the shops) are closed
karai deshou?	-	It's spicy, right?
zembu nai	-	They are all gone
baikin ga tsuiteru, kao ni	-	There are germs, on your face
e? doushite?	-	Eh? Why?
hoshi mo dete kuru	-	The stars will come out too

---

[1] Should be '*Okaasan mitsuketa*' (Mummy found it), since '*Okaasan sagashita*' would mean 'Mummy searched'.
[2] Should be '*Baaba to Jiiji no toki wa te arawanakatta*'.
[3] '*tomodachi*' means 'friend' or 'acquaintance', but young children refer to all other children as '*otomodachi*'.

Day 3

asa ni natta kara hon yomu?	-	It is morning now so shall we read a book?
minna moratta n desu ka?	-	Did everyone get one?
shashin torimasu ka?	-	Will you take a photo?
minna no shashin totte ii?	-	Can I take everyone's photo?
minna kigaeru kara chotto matte	-	Everyone is changing so please wait a minute
minna kigaeteru nee	-	Everyone is changing, aren't they?
Minnie-chan tasukemasu	-	I will rescue Minnie Mouse
watashi itte kuru	-	I'm off now
Minnie-chan totte kita	-	I fetched Minnie Mouse
mazui desu	-	It tastes bad
taberu hito?	-	Who wants to eat some? / Anyone want to eat some?
asa ni nattenai kara, yoru dakara nenne shite ii yo	-	It isn't morning yet, so it's still night, so you can sleep[4]
T-kun ni kawarimasu	-	I will pass you to T-kun (on the phone)
Otousan wa yonjus-sai	-	Daddy is 40 years old
A-chan nansai dakke?	-	How old is A-chan again?
san-sai desu	-	She is three years old

Notes

> A-chan replies correctly to negative questions, which tend to be the opposite way around to English. For example, in reply to '*tabenai?*' (Won't you eat it?) she might say '*hai*' to mean 'No I won't'. Although '*hai*' literally means 'Yes', here it means 'Yes that is correct that I won't eat it'. It is also common to avoid 'yes' and 'no' altogether and repeat the verb in the reply instead. For example, when asked '*kore tabenai?*' (Won't you eat it?), you can

---

[4] The Japanese here is just as awkward as the English.

say '*tabenai*' (I won't eat it) or '*taberu*' (I will eat it). You can also say '*hai, tabenai*' (No, I won't eat it).

Day 4

Otousan shawaa ni itte ii yo	-	Daddy, you can go and have a shower[5]
oishisou tte itteru	-	He says it looks tasty
yooguruto tabete ii?	-	Can I eat yogurt?
omutsu de itte ii?	-	Can I go there in my nappy?
Shima-chan owattara kyoukai ni iku	-	I will go to church when Shima-chan finishes
kore to onaji dakara kuro ni shiyou	-	It's the same as this so let's have the black one
hai, tsugi wa Otousan desu	-	Okay, Daddy is next
koko mo shimatteru no?	-	Is this one (shop) closed too?
Shima-chan hamigaki shinai n datte	-	They say Shima-chan doesn't brush his teeth
ookikunattara toreru kara Otousan totte	-	I will be able to reach it when I get bigger, so Daddy please get it
A-chan ima ookii desu	-	A-chan is big right now
Baikinman kowai hito	-	Baikinman is a scary person[6]
tsugi wa dore ga ii?	-	Which one shall we do next?
densha notte, osembei tabeyou yo	-	Let's get on the train and eat rice crackers
arukeru	-	I can walk
chuu shitara dame	-	You mustn't kiss me
dare mo inai desu ka?	-	Isn't anyone there?
kudasai, kore	-	Please give it to me, this one
aratte kita	-	I went and washed them

Day 5

mukae ni konai de	-	Don't come to pick me up

---

[5] Literally 'Daddy, you can go to the shower'.
[6] Baikinman is the adversary of the character Anpanman.

aka dakara ikanai	-	It's red so we won't go[7]
hashittara koronjau	-	If you run you will fall over
mukou de kigaeru	-	I will dress over there / I will change clothes when we get there
tomodachi to te o tsunaida	-	I held hands with my friends[8]
chotto mite ii n desu ka?	-	May I watch a little bit? / May I have a quick look?
haitta	-	I got it in / They went in / I got them on (socks etc)
kore wakaranai	-	I don't know this
atode nomu	-	I will drink it later

Day 6

A-chan hitori de itte ii?	-	Can A-chan go by herself?
osoto mieru	-	I can see outside
kaerou	-	Let's go home
Okaasan onaka ni akachan ga iru	-	There is a baby in Mummy's tummy
akachan ookikunattara juusu to miruku ageru	-	When the baby gets big I will give it juice and milk
akachan umareru	-	The baby will be born
minna okichau	-	Everyone will wake up
takusan nonjatta?	-	Did you drink a lot?
totchatta	-	I took them off
kakuretenai	-	He isn't hiding

Day 7

Otousan konnichi wa shite ii yo	-	Daddy you can say hello
kore moraitai	-	I want to keep this
maa ii ya, kore ni suru	-	Oh well, I'll have this one
moretenai n desu	-	It hasn't leaked
kudasai yo!	-	Give it to me, please!

---

[7] At traffic lights.
[8] A-chan now uses particle '*o*' in '*te o tsunaida*' (I held hands).

A-chan fuitenai	-	A-chan hasn't wiped it
fukanai	-	I won't wipe it
dakara dame	-	So that's no good / That's why it's no good
dore de mo ii	-	Any one will do / Any one is okay

Common mistakes

onaji miru	-	I will watch the same one[9]

Day 8

kawaita yo	-	It's dry / It has dried
kore wa kawaitenai	-	This hasn't dried
A-chan no tegami	-	A-chan's letter
biribiri shinai de	-	Don't rip it[10]
tatte yaranai to	-	You have to do it standing up
minna iru?	-	Are they all there?
S-chan to gotsun shichatta	-	I bumped into S-chan
chigau, M-chan to S-chan kenka shite, Anpanman to koronjatta	-	No, M-chan argued with S-chan, and fell down with Anpanman

Day 9

jibun de oriru	-	I will get down by myself
hayaku shigoto ikanai to	-	You have to go to work quickly / You have to hurry off to work
mitsukatchatta	-	I was found / You found me
ashita hoikuen yasumi dakara ikanai	-	Tomorrow is a holiday at nursery school so I won't go
a, mata denki?	-	Ah, the lights again?
Otousan ga doa aketara oto ga shita	-	There was a noise when Daddy opened the door
datte koko de yaru no	-	Well, because I will do it here

---

[9] Should be '*onaji no miru*'.
[10] '*biribiri*' is the sound of ripping, but in children's speech it is used as a verb.

A-chan youfuku ni Otousan ga pe tte yatta	-	Daddy spat on A-chan's clothes

Day 10

doko desu ka?	-	Where is it?
doko da yo?!	-	Where is it?!
akachan ga nenne shiteru no, Okaasan no onaka ni	-	The baby is sleeping, in Mummy's stomach
itai desu yo	-	This is going to hurt
watashi ga torou ka?	-	Shall I fetch it?
Jingle Bells minna utatte ne	-	Everyone sing Jingle Bells, alright?
dame da	-	It's no good
tonderu	-	I'm flying
kamera ga kitchatta	-	The camera went off
kesou	-	Let's delete it / Let's erase it

Common mistakes

dareka ochichatta	-	Someone dropped it[11]

Day 11

kinou M-chan to karee tabeta	-	Yesterday we ate curry with M-chan
chotto iro ga chigau	-	The colours are a bit different
ryoute de yatte	-	Do it with both hands
nakanakatta	-	I didn't cry
taorechatta	-	I fell over
mukae ni kuru to	-	When you come to pick me up

Day 12

a, wasurechatta n deshou?	-	Ah, you've forgotten, right?
shashin torou yo	-	Let's take photos
atama ga ugoku	-	Her head moves

---

[11] Should be '*otoshichatta*' (dropped it), since '*ochichatta*' would mean 'fell down'.

mada yaiteru	-	I'm still cooking them[12]
yakanai	-	I won't toast it
itsumo kore desu	-	It's always this one

Day 13

Cinderella oryouri suru	-	Cinderella will do the cooking[13]
kaette kitara yaru no	-	I'll do it when we come back home
minna isshoni, itadakimasu!	-	Everyone together, let's eat!
chotto matte, kore mitai no	-	Wait a minute, I want to see this
nan no oto?	-	What was that noise?
kuro no sokkusu	-	The black socks

Day 14

Otousan omocha mottenai desu	-	Daddy doesn't have any toys
zembu tabeta kara okawari suru	-	I ate it all so I will have another helping
Okaasan osoi kara saki ni gohan tabeyou ka?	-	Mummy is late so shall we eat dinner first?
okoranai de	-	Don't get angry
zembu ii naa	-	They are all nice

Day 15

mata atode kite ii yo	-	You can come again later
sou nan da?	-	Is that right?[14]
naosanai to	-	We'll have to fix it
watashi ga okotteru yo!	-	I am angry! / I'm the one to be angry!
M-chan hoikuen ni konakatta no	-	M-chan didn't come to nursery school

---

[12] 'yaku' means to 'cook', 'bake', 'toast', 'grill' etc, or 'to burn'.
[13] The honorific 'o' in 'oryouri' is frequently dropped.
[14] 'nan da' here is a contraction of 'na no desu' (feminine speech for 'is'), however 'nan da' is not feminine speech.

Day 16

ii no	-	That's alright
omizu nai no, dakara motte kite	-	There's no water, so bring some
mada asa ja nai	-	It isn't morning yet
atama ki o tsukete	-	Mind your head
Baaba to Jiiji mo kita	-	Grandma and Grandpa came too
kore tabetara kouhii nomou ne	-	Let's drink coffee after we eat this, okay?

Day 17

doa shimete	-	Close the door
suwatte, koko ni	-	Sit down, here
wakarimashita	-	I understand / Okay
irimasu	-	I want it / I need it
kurakunatta kara mabushikunai	-	It has become dark so it isn't bright
Otousan to odoritai	-	I want to dance with Daddy

Day 18

A-chan fuitara yada!	-	I don't want you to wipe A-chan!
chanto motte nomu no?	-	Will you hold it properly and drink it?
nani ga koko ni haitteru ka naa?	-	I wonder what is inside here?
tabun ne	-	Probably
hitotsu me ga aru, hitotsu nai	-	He has one eye, one is missing

Day 19

doa shimenasai!	-	Close the door!
sorosoro ikanakya	-	I have to go soon / I've gotta go soon[15]
mada da yo!	-	Not yet!

---

[15] The '*-nakya*' form of a verb is quite colloquial.

kyou wa Otousan oshigoto itchau yo	-	Today Daddy will go off to work[16]
takusan asobou	-	Let's play lots

Notes

> A-chan is able to count to 12: *ichi, ni, san, shi* (or *yon*), *go, roku, nana* (or *shichi*), *hachi, kyuu, juu, juuichi, juuni*

Day 20

atchi wa dame	-	That's the wrong way / Don't go that way
kowareteta no?	-	Was it broken?
kore miru no?	-	Are we going to watch this?
oto ga kowai	-	The noise is scary
otoshitara kowarechau	-	It will break if you drop it

Day 21

Otousan gomi sutete kuru no?	-	Is Daddy going to throw the rubbish out?
ame dakara, kasa mottenai to nurechau kara, motte ikimasu	-	It's rain, so we'll get wet if we don't have an umbrella, so I'll take one[17]
pajama dasu	-	I will get my pajamas out
chotto kao ga mienai	-	I can't quite see your face
ochitsuite	-	Calm down
A-chan sugu kaette kichau yo	-	A-chan will come home soon
jaketto nugitai	-	I want to take off my jacket
minna de itadakimashou	-	Let's all eat together

Common mistakes

Otousan ga kimatte	-	Daddy you decide[18]

---

[16] The honorific '*o*' in '*oshigoto*' is frequently dropped.
[17] The Japanese here is just as awkward as the English.
[18] Should be '*Otousan ga kimete*' (Daddy you decide). A-chan is confusing '*kimeru*' (to decide) with '*kimaru*' (to be decided).

Day 22

futari to mo ookii	-	They are both big people[19]
doa shimetai	-	I want to close the door
yaranakatta	-	I didn't do it
shita	-	I did it
yatta	-	I did it
nezumi-san ga ouma-san ni natta	-	The mice turned into horses
demo ouji-sama ga iru	-	But the prince is there
datte, mada kigaetenai desu	-	Well, because I haven't dressed yet

Day 23

A-chan saki ni nonjau wa	-	A-chan will drink first
tabun futtenai ja nai?	-	It's probably not raining, is it?
me tsubutte	-	Close your eyes
me tsubutte tte itteru	-	She says close your eyes
kowakunai, yasashii no	-	He isn't scary, he's kind[20]
sakki Okaasan katazukechatta	-	Mummy put them away a little while ago
te ga kirei ja nai naa	-	My hands aren't clean, are they
akerenai	-	I can't open it[21]

Day 24

Okaasan ga itteta n deshou?	-	Mummy was saying that, right?
dame, dame, jibun no ja nai deshou?	-	No, no, it isn't yours, right?
guchagucha	-	It's all messed up / It's all soggy
I-chan no akachan ga umarechatta	-	I-chan's baby was born
futa shimenai to taihen da yo	-	It will be terrible if you don't close the lid

---

[19] Literally 'The two people are both big'.
[20] '*kowai*' can mean 'scared' or 'scary', so '*kowakunai*' means 'not scared' or 'not scary'.
[21] '*akerenai*' is a contraction of '*akerarenai*' (can't open).

R-chan ni omocha miseru	-	I will show the toys to R-chan
watashi wa koko ga ii	-	I like it here / I will stay here
dare desu ka?	-	Who is it?

Day 25

tsugi wa kasa mou chotto hiraku	-	Next we will open the umbrella a little more
hiraite, hiraite	-	Open it, open it
tojite yaru	-	I will do it with it closed
koko ni suwatte yaru	-	I will sit here and do it
A-chan ouchi de matteru kara mada ikanai	-	A-chan is waiting at home so we won't go yet
te tsunagou	-	Let's hold hands
chotto baggu ni ireyou ka na	-	Let's just put it in the bag, shall we
hito ga kichau kara hayaku baggu ni irenai to	-	We have to put it in the bag before someone comes along[22]
mou chotto de soto da yo	-	Soon we will be outside[23]
A-chan to Okaasan hikouki de gohan taberu	-	A-chan and Mummy will have their meal on the plane
a, kuruma kichatta	-	Ah, a car has come / Ah, a car is coming
A-chan mou orichau	-	A-chan will get off now
hashiranai to	-	We will have to run
kyou wa Okaasan to ofuro desu	-	Today bath is with Mummy
kyou wa Okaasan to ofuro hairu	-	Today I will have a bath with Mummy
Otousan to hairanai	-	I won't get in with Daddy
mou chotto doa shimenai to	-	We must close the door a bit more

Day 26

doa don to shita deshou?	-	You banged the door, right?

---

[22] Literally 'People will come along so we must put it in the bag quickly'.
[23] Literally 'In a little bit, it will be outside'. On a train that went both underground and overground.

Three years: Month two

Otousan doa shimenasai, A-chan kagi motteru kara	-	Daddy you must close the door, because A-chan has the key
kenka shitenai	-	We haven't argued
A-chan ga dasu	-	A-chan will put them out
dete kuru n ja nai?	-	It will come out, won't it?
mou nai n ja nai?	-	There aren't any more, are there?
omoshiroi n ja nai?	-	It's fun, isn't it?
eeto, eeto...	-	Um, um...
Okaasan dame datte	-	Mummy says no
mada A-chan ga isshoukenmei yattemasu kara, atode asobimasu	-	A-chan is still trying very hard, so we will play later
konai de	-	Don't come
katai nee	-	It's hard, isn't it
A-chan dekiru n ja nai?	-	A-chan can do it, can't she?
abunai n ja nai?	-	It's dangerous, isn't it?
Otousan no me tabetenai ja nai?	-	I'm not eating Daddy's eye, am I?

Common mistakes

dansu no koko ni inai	-	She is not in this dance[24]

Day 27

Okaasan no hou ni ikitai	-	I want to go over to Mummy[25]
Buzz A-chan no baggu ni haitchatta	-	Buzz went into A-chan's bag
Otousan omizu iranai n ja nai?	-	Daddy doesn't want water, does he?
itakunai n ja nai?	-	It doesn't hurt, does it?
nanika mieru?	-	Can you see something?
Okaasan mo moraitakatta tte	-	Mummy said she wanted to get one too[26]
ato wa dame desu	-	Not the rest / You can't have the rest

---

[24] Should be '*kono dansu ni denai*'.
[25] '*no hou*' literally means 'in the direction of'.
[26] The trailing '*tte*' here implies '*tte itta*' (said).

kore wa owattenai n desu	-	This hasn't finished
juusu moraeru	-	We can get juice / They will give us juice
kono hito dare?	-	Who is this person?
ouchi ni... nan dakke?... motte konakatta	-	I didn't bring... what was it?... it's at home
ookii yatsu	-	The big one[27]

Common mistakes

pikapika shite n ja nai?	-	It's flashing, isn't it?[28]
kou yatte ja nai kara	-	Because you don't do it like this[29]
onaka kakurete	-	Hide your stomach[30]

Day 28

korokoro	-	Rolling
kireta	-	It snapped / It broke off
Shirayuki-hime ouma-san ni notta	-	Snow White rode on the horse[31]
megane toranai to	-	You have to take off your glasses
ima kami ga nai nee	-	Now you don't have any hair, do you?
kikoeta?	-	Did you hear that?
dare ga dashita no?	-	Who got it out? / Who put it out?
Okaasan ni miseru	-	I will show Mummy
minna mawatte kudasai	-	Everyone spin around please
minna Okaasan to Otousan to yarimashou	-	Let's all do it with Mummy and Daddy

---

[27] '*yatsu*' is literally a derogatory term for 'guy', but here it is used as a slang term for 'thing'.
[28] Should be '*chikachika*' (flashing), not '*pikapika*' (sparkling).
[29] Should be '*kou yatte yaru n ja nai*' or '*kou yaranai kara*'.
[30] Should be '*onaka kakushite*'.
[31] '*-hime*' means 'princess', so Snow White is literally called 'Princess Snow White'.

Day 29

hadaka dakara	-	Because I'm naked
kou ja nai	-	Not like this[32]
nanka wakaranai nee	-	You don't really get it, do you?
kiiro ni shimashou	-	Let's have the yellow one
tabun kowarechau	-	It will probably break
ikko nai	-	There is one missing / One is missing
kowai hito ga imashita	-	There was a scary person[33]
Okaasan no tonari ga ii	-	I want to be next to Mummy

Day 30

Otousan ga oite itchatta	-	Daddy left it behind
kasa iru	-	We will need umbrellas[34]
matte n no!	-	I'm waiting!
oite ku	-	I will leave it behind[35]
tabun kore ja nai?	-	It's probably this one, isn't it?
hayaku yarimashou	-	Let's do it quickly / Quickly, let's do it
chiisaku yarimashou	-	Let's make it small
tetsudai shite	-	Help me with it
ame mou yanda	-	It's already stopped raining / The rain has stopped now
minna mou nuretenai	-	Everyone is dry now[36]
kyou nagagutsu ni suru no?	-	Will we have the boots today?
ohana ga saiteru	-	The flowers are blooming

---

[32] The meaning is the opposite when posed as a question: '*kou ja nai?*' (It's like this, isn't it?).

[33] A-chan uses the polite '*-mashita*' form here because she is pretending to read a book.

[34] '*iru*' here means 'need' instead of 'want'.

[35] '*oite ku*' is a contraction of '*oite iku*', which is from '*oku*' (to put) and '*iku*' (to go). So it literally means 'I will leave it and go'.

[36] Literally 'Everyone is not wet anymore' or 'Everyone is already not wet'.

Day 31

T-kun shinkansen de kaetchatta	-	T-kun went back by bullet train
mou denai?	-	Has it all come out?[37]
nanka haitte n ja nai?	-	There's something in there, isn't there?
yappari kiiro ni shiyou	-	Let's make it the yellow one after all
koko ni haittara dame	-	You mustn't come in here
irechatta deshou?	-	You put it in, right?
Minnie-chan wa oitoku	-	I will leave Minnie Mouse (doll)
A-chan sakki asondeta yo	-	A-chan was playing with it just before
Otousan mo sagashite	-	Daddy, you look for it too

---

[37] Literally 'It won't come out anymore?' or 'It already won't come out?'.

Three years: Month three

Day 1

nande Ariel ni shita?	-	Why did you choose Ariel?
denki tsukeyou yo, koko	-	Let's turn on the lights, in here
Otousan gambatte aruita	-	Daddy walked the whole way / Daddy did his best to walk
nande morawanakatta, nee?	-	Why didn't you get one?

Common mistakes

dareka nottenai kara	-	Because nobody is riding on it[1]

Day 2

Shima-chan no pazuru kudasai	-	Please give me the Shima-chan jigsaw
shiroi gohan ga ii	-	I want white rice
mou sorosoro okichau	-	She will get up soon
kore wa nan desu ka ne?	-	What is this, then?

Day 3

saki ni omocha	-	The toys first
a, sokka?	-	Oh, really? / Is that so?[2]
Otousan ga kimete	-	Daddy, you decide
Okaasan to iku	-	I will go with Mummy

Day 4

Okaasan ga motteru	-	Mummy has it
miru dake	-	We will just watch
Ariel dake	-	Just Ariel
doushita no?	-	What happened?

---

[1] Should be '*dare mo nottenai kara*'.
[2] '*sokka*' is a contraction of '*sou ka*' (Is that so?).

Day 5

A-chan mitai!	-	A-chan wants to see! / A-chan wants to watch!
hai, arigatou gozaimasu!	-	Okay, thank you very much!
kuchi ga aru kara tabechau yo	-	It has a mouth so it will eat you
chotto tsukurimasu	-	I'll just make it / I'll make a little bit

Day 6

gohan ni kaketara dame desu	-	You mustn't put it on your rice
eee? wakaru no, watashi no uchi?	-	Eh? Do you know my house?
kikoemasen	-	I can't hear it

Common mistakes

mada yaketeru no	-	I'm still cooking it[3]
yaketa yo!	-	I cooked it![4]
ikko dake nai	-	There is only one[5]
Otousan ga tsuichatta	-	Daddy put it on[6]

Day 7

mou aketara dame	-	You mustn't open it anymore
mukou wa samui deshou?	-	It's cold over there, right?
kowaresou dakara	-	It looks breakable, so... (be careful)
yappari kowai	-	I am scared after all

Day 8

doushite wakaranai no?	-	Why don't you understand?
ikimashou ka?	-	Shall we go?
Rika-chan no hou ni iru	-	She's over by Licca-chan
dare kara moratta n dakke?	-	Who did I get it from again?

---

[3] Should be '*mada yaiteru no*'.
[4] Should be '*yaita*' (I cooked it), not '*yaketa*' (It cooked).
[5] Should be '*ikko shika nai*' or '*ikko dake shika nai*'.
[6] Should be '*tsukechatta*' (put on), not '*tsuichatta*' (got on).

shibaraku aenai	- We won't be able to meet them again for a while
jaa, tabeyou	- Well then, let's eat[7]
oshikko deta to omou	- I think wee has come out

"*dechatta*" – It came out...

Day 9

Minnie-chan mo tabetai tte itta	- Minnie Mouse said she wants to eat too
nanika ochichatta no	- Something fell down
Otousan shigoto ni iku no?	- Daddy are you going to work?
asa Okaasan to Otousan okitara, miruku nonde, mukae ni iku	- In the morning when Mummy and Daddy get up, they will drink milk, and go to pick them up
kuruma ga kichau kara, koko ni haitchatte	- Cars are coming, so come in here
obake ouchi ni konai	- Ghosts won't come to our house
kuttsuiteru kara, dakara dame	- They are stuck together, so that's why it's no good[8]
kore de ii?	- Will this do?

Common mistakes

jitensha kowarete naoshiteru	- The bicycle broke so he's fixing it[9]

---

[7] '*jaa*' here is the same as '*ja*' (well / then).

[8] Having both '*kara*' and '*dakara*' is technically redundant, but in speech can be used to add emphasis.

[9] Should be '*jitensha kowareta kara naoshiteru*'.

Notes

> A-chan likes to make her sentences as long as possible. She now joins phrases using '-*tara*', '*kara*', and the '-*te*' form of verbs.

Day 10

sou nan da!	-	That's right![10]
doko na no?	-	Where are you? / Where is it?[11]
kore mo oite ikanai to	-	I have to leave this here too
mou hitori inai deshou?	-	One other person is missing, right? / There isn't another person, right?[12]
koko dake	-	Just here / Only here
pinku no onigiri setto mieta	-	I've spotted a pink rice-balls set meal[13]

Day 11

te tsunagitakatta	-	I wanted to hold hands
kotchi no te	-	This hand[14]
botan yaritakatta	-	I wanted to do the buttons
isu wa kitchin ni aru	-	The chair is in the kitchen
mou owari na no	-	It's already the end
hon kaeshichatta no	-	We took the books back / We returned the books
saki ni nomanai de	-	Don't drink before us / Don't drink it first
isshoni nomu kara	-	Because we will drink together
nuganai yo	-	I won't undress
dareka funjatta	-	Someone stood on it
ao, etou... nan dakke? shikaku	-	A blue, ah... what is it again?, a square

---

[10] Compare this with '*sou nan da?*' (Is that right?), seen previously.
[11] Remember '*na no*' used like this is feminine speech.
[12] '*mou hitori*' means 'one more person'.
[13] Literally 'I could see...' since '*mieta*' is past tense.
[14] Literally 'The hand on this side'.

tsukareta wa!	-	I'm tired![15]

Common mistakes

yada deshou?	-	It's horrible, right?[16]

Day 12

kore wa mou owatchatta	-	This has finished already
kirei datta?	-	Was it pretty? / Were they clean?
arimashita yo!	-	Here it is! / I found it!
kore wa ryouhou motte	-	Hold both of these
basu ni norimashou	-	Let's take the bus / Let's get on the bus
ima totte kuru	-	I will go and get it now

Day 13

kyou Baaba no uchi ni, Okaasan to Otousan to iku	-	Today I will go to Grandma's house, with Mummy and Daddy
Otousan, asa da yo! okinasai! to itte kuru	-	I'll go and say, Daddy, it's morning! Get up!
hora!	-	Look!
kore wa dare no datta?	-	Whose was this?
dare no doresu ni shiyou?	-	Whose dress shall we have?
Minnie-chan asobitai n datte	-	Minnie Mouse says she wants to play
kore kara, kore yarou	-	Next, let's do this[17]
ano hito seki deta	-	That person coughed
motto ookiku!	-	Bigger!
suberidai isshoni yaritakatta kara	-	Because I wanted to go on the slide together

---

[15] Remember the trailing '*wa*' is feminine speech.
[16] '*yada*' is a contraction of '*iya da*', so '*da*' is redundant here since both '*da*' and '*deshou*' are forms of '*desu*'. It should be '*iya deshou?*' (It's horrible, right?) or '*yada ne?*' (It's horrible, isn't it?).
[17] '*kore kara*' (after this) can also mean 'from now on'.

Common mistakes

chiisai no Buzz, doko?	-	Where is the small Buzz Lightyear?[18]
ookii no kooen	-	The big park[19]

Day 14

mukou ni iru	-	She's over there
nani mo kangaetenai	-	I haven't thought about anything
nondara iku no	-	I'll go when I have drunk this
kore mo aru	-	There is this too / We have these too

Common mistakes

hadaka konai de	-	Don't come naked[20]

Day 15

Otousan koppu ni omizu iretara dame deshou?	-	Daddy shouldn't put water in the cup, right?
Okaasan ga tsukaitakatta deshou?	-	Mummy wanted to use it, right?
jaketto kurokunatta kara kirenai	-	The jacket's gone black so I can't wear it
botan wa mae datta?	-	Did the buttons go at the front?
zembu moratchau no?	-	Are we going to keep them all?
tonakai-san konai to omou, Santa-san dake	-	I don't think the reindeer will come, just Santa
Minnie-chan mo mitakatta	-	Minnie Mouse wanted to see too[21]

Day 16

nokoshitenai	-	I haven't left any
mada yo	-	Not yet[22]

---

[18] Should be '*chiisai Buzz, doko?*'.
[19] Should be '*ookii kooen*'.
[20] Should be '*hadaka de konai de*'.
[21] This phrase could also mean 'I wanted to see Minnie Mouse too'.
[22] Remember '*yo*' without '*da*' is feminine speech.

kotchi mo mae -	This one goes at the front too[23]
akachan mada chiisai no -	The baby is still small
atashi nee, eeto... -	Me, well, um...

Common mistakes

mou ikkai no botan atta -	There was one more button[24]

Day 17

don to shitara dame -	You mustn't bang it
yasashiku! -	Gently!
unchi detara pantsu hakou nee -	Let's put my underpants on when I have done poos
Okaasan to yarou -	Let's do it with Mummy
kore yarou ne -	Let's do this, shall we?
dakko shite mitai -	I want you to hold me while I watch[25]

Day 18

A-chan mukou ni iku kara shawaa shinasai! -	A-chan will go over there, so take a shower!
nagakunatchatta -	It got longer / It became long
hitori de ikanai -	I won't go by myself
minna de itta -	Everyone went together / We all went

Day 19

A-chan wa hadaka! -	A-chan is naked!
gomen! -	Sorry!
ooki na koe -	A loud voice[26]
ookiku, motto -	Bigger, even more
atode doresu kiru no -	I will wear the dress later

---

[23] '*kotchi*' here means 'this one', rather than 'here'.
[24] Should be '*mou ikko no botan atta*'.
[25] Literally 'I want to hug and watch'.
[26] '*ookii*' becomes '*ooki*' when followed by '*na*'.

Day 20

Okaasan mou ofuro	- Mummy's already in the bath
M-chan ga seki ga naotta	- M-chan's cough got better
dotchi ga ookii ka na?	- I wonder which is bigger?
dotchi ga chiisai?	- Which is smaller?

Day 21

te tsunaideru	- They are holding hands
hito ga inai kara	- Because there are no people
dame da yo nee	- That's bad, isn't it
suteki!	- Lovely!

Day 22

mou kawaita	- It's dry already
ochinai de tte itteru no	- I'm saying don't fall off
sugokatta	- It was amazing
atama ni tsuiteru yo	- It's stuck on your head
kataguruma to onaji da yo	- It's the same as a shoulder-ride
kirei ni naru yo	- You will become pretty / It will make you beautiful

Day 23

hantai no hou ni	- On the opposite side
yubi hasanjatta	- My finger got caught
ima ne, yubi de yatteru	- Now, you see, I'm doing it with my finger
mada asa da yo	- It's still morning

Common mistakes

dare de mo inakatta	- Nobody was there[27]
M-chan Shirayuki-hime kashita	- M-chan lent me Snow White[28]

---

[27] Should be '*dare mo inakatta*'.
[28] Should be '*M-chan Shirayuki-hime kashite kureta*'.

Three years: Month three 153

hikouki suwatteru	- The plane is stopped[29]

Day 24

ouchi ni oni ga konai yo	- The ogres won't come to our home
Okaasan wa inai to omou	- I think Mummy is not there
Minnie-chan ga inakatta	- Minnie Mouse wasn't there
Okaasan ni oshiete kuru	- I will go and let Mummy know

Day 25

dakko shite yaritai	- I want you to carry me while I do it
pasokon yatte imasen	- I'm not doing the computer
chotto hen	- It's a bit strange
okane irenai to	- You have to put money in it
ano ne...	- Excuse me...
ima haihai shiteru no	- I am crawling now

Day 26

A-chan wa kutsu yatte n no!	- A-chan is doing her shoes!
E-chan atode kuru no	- E-chan will come later
Otousan no hiza ni	- On Daddy's knees
kore de iku?	- Will you go in this?
ikko dake ramune tabetai	- I just want to eat one lemonade sweet

Day 27

Jiiji to yatte ne, futari to mo	- Do it with Grandpa, both of you
modoshite	- Put it back
modoshinasai!	- Put it back!
yubi sasanai de	- Don't point your finger

---

[29] Should be '*hikouki tomatteru*' (The plane is stopped), since '*hikouki suwatteru*' would mean 'The plane is sitting'.

Day 28

shita ni aru yo	-	It's downstairs
unten shiteru	-	He is driving
yamenasai!	-	Stop it!
itakatta deshou	-	It hurt, right? / It must have hurt

Three years: Month four

Day 1

hontou ni?	-	Really?
hontou ni ka naa?	-	Really, I wonder?
umaretemasen	-	He/she is not born yet
hadashi de ikanai	-	I won't go barefoot
mou itakunai	-	It doesn't hurt anymore
koko de matte	-	Wait here

Day 2

Otousan wa koko de matte te	-	Daddy you wait here
Otousan hirotte yo	-	Daddy, pick it up
D-san iru to ii naa	-	I hope D-san will be there[1]
dore ni shiyou ka naa?	-	Which one shall I have?
aa! kore ni suru	-	Ah! I'll have this one
futari to mo douzo	-	Go ahead, both of you

Day 3

hadashi de soto ittara dame	-	You mustn't go outside barefoot
mukou de matteru kara	-	They are waiting for you there (so...)
ippai yaranai de ne	-	Don't do it a lot / Don't do it too much
kyou Okaasan to asonda	-	Today I played with Mummy
ii desu yo	-	That's okay
Okaasan, doko ni iru no?	-	Mummy, where are you?

Day 4

Okaasan, osoi naa to itta, Otousan ga	-	Mummy, Daddy said you're late aren't you
a! nanka funderu	-	Ah! You're treading on something

---

[1] '*to ii*' means 'I hope'.

A-chan toire ni Okaasan to ikou	-	A-chan will go to the toilet with Mummy[2]
Mickey ga hantai da	-	Mickey Mouse is on backwards
dakko shite mo ii yo	-	You can carry me
panpan	-	Pat, pat[3]

Day 5

kyou jabajaba ni D-san ga kuru	-	Today D-san will come swimming[4]
kusuguttai deshou?	-	It tickles, right?
ato de hirou	-	I'll pick it up later
omawarisan ni tsukamatchau kara Otousan to ikanai to	-	You have to go with Daddy or you will be arrested by a policeman
yooguruto tabete mo ii n desu ka?	-	May I eat yogurt?

Day 6

hazukashikatta	-	It was embarrassing / I was embarrassed
chigau heya ni iku yo	-	I will go to a different room
beruto shite, A-chan no	-	Do the seat-belt, A-chan's one
omutsu de shitenakatta	-	I hadn't done it in my nappy

Notes

> Compare these common negative verb forms and their more formal equivalents:

shinai	-	won't	-	*shimasen*
shinakatta	-	didn't	-	*shimasen deshita*
shitenai	-	am not / aren't / haven't	-	*shite imasen*
shitenakatta	-	wasn't / weren't / hadn't	-	*shite imasen deshita*

---

[2] Literally 'let's go' ('*ikou*'). In English we might say 'Mummy, let's go to the toilet together'.

[3] '*panpan*' is the sound of patting, slapping or smacking. A-chan used it here as she brushed the soles of her feet.

[4] Remember '*jabajaba*' is a children's word.

Day 7

kuroi yatsu	-	The black one
atchi kara ga ii	-	From over there would be good
chotto miteru dake	-	Just having a quick look
nakusanai de	-	Don't lose it
kore mo nakusanai	-	We won't lose this either
omatase!	-	Thank you for waiting![5]

Day 8

zembu nonjatta no, Okaasan?	-	Did you drink it all, Mummy?
mada haitteru ja nai?	-	Isn't there still some in it?
pindome katte koyou nee	-	Let's go and buy a hair pin
mou daijoubu	-	It's okay now
isshoni tabeteru no	-	We are eating together
akerenakunatchatta	-	I can't open it anymore[6]

Day 9

nagete ii?	-	Can I throw it?
koko ni shiyou ka?	-	Shall we go here? / How about here?
gohan wasuretara dame da yo	-	We mustn't forget the rice
Okaasan kitchin ni inakatta yo	-	Mummy wasn't in the kitchen
kou shite yatte n no!	-	I'm doing it like this!
anata wa koko	-	You stay here

Day 10

pinku ni shita yo nee	-	You chose the pink one, didn't you
motto tabenai	-	I won't eat more
demo ne, watashitachi wa kimerenai	-	But you see, we can't decide[7]
jibun ga motte te tabete	-	Hold it yourself and eat it

---

[5] '*omatase*' is short for '*omatase shimashita*' (Thank you for waiting).
[6] Literally 'It has become unable to be opened'.
[7] '*kimerenai*' is a contraction of '*kimerarenai*' (can't decide).

Common mistakes

akai yatsu no pantsu ga ii	-	I want the red underpants[8]

Day 11

mou kimechatta	-	I have already decided
kore ni shita no	-	I chose this
urusai!	-	Shut up! / You're a nuisance![9]
watashi aruite ikanai	-	I won't walk there
zubon ni kuttsuichatta	-	They got stuck on my trousers

Day 12

kore sanko	-	This makes three / This is the third one
kore yaranai to	-	We have to do this
youfuku ni koboshichatta yo	-	I spilled it on my clothes
ikkai orite ii yo	-	You can get off briefly / You can get down once
D-san no T-shatsu to onaji datta	-	It was the same as D-san's T-shirt
Okaasan, soujiki owatta?	-	Mummy, are you finished vacuuming?

Day 13

kou shite yaritakatta	-	I wanted to do it like this
juusu nomitai wa	-	I want to drink juice
oriyou	-	Let's get off
atashi motte kuru wa	-	I'll bring it[10]
nagenai de yo!	-	Don't throw it!
otetsudai shinai de	-	Don't help me

---

[8] Should be '*akai pantsu ga ii*' (I want the red underpants) or '*akai yatsu ga ii*' (I want the red ones).
[9] '*urusai*' literally means 'noisy' or 'annoying'.
[10] Remember both '*atashi*' and trailing '*wa*' are feminine speech.

Day 14

itchatte	-	Off you go
ikimasu	-	I will go
ima ikimasu!	-	I will go now!
mou toranai de	-	Don't take any more
kore jaa shite	-	Wash this away[11]
jaa shite	-	Flush it

Common mistakes

ue ni naite ikitai	-	I want to go upstairs and cry[12]

Day 15

watashi saki	-	Me first
futari to mo koko de nani shiteru no?	-	What are the two of you doing here?
atarashii no, kudasai	-	Please give me a new one
Genie no mane shiteru	-	I'm pretending to be Genie / I'm copying Genie
Genie no mane datta	-	It was an imitation of Genie

Common mistakes

minna no kore dakara ne	-	Because this is everyone's[13]

Day 16

kaette kitara kore kiru yo nee	-	I'll wear this when we get home, won't I?
Otousan ga ii yo tte ittara ii	-	It's okay if Daddy says it's okay
kotchi ni oitoku	-	I will leave it here
isoide	-	Hurry
hayaku, isoide	-	Quick, hurry

---

[11] '*jaa*' (じゃー) used as a verb is a children's word meaning 'wash away' or 'flush'.
[12] Should be '*ue ni itte nakitai*'.
[13] Should be '*kore wa minna no dakara ne*'.

Day 17

chotto chiisai	-	It's a bit small
ame ga yanda	-	The rain has stopped
kore tsukawanakute ii yo nee	-	I don't have to use this, do I?
DVD kuruma de minakatta	-	I didn't watch a DVD in the car

Day 18

kore wa kuma-chan ga kiru	-	The teddy bear will wear this
kinou wa ame futtenakatta	-	Yesterday it wasn't raining
kore de ii deshou?	-	This is okay, right?
ugoitara yaru	-	I'll do it if it moves / I'll do it when it moves
tataku yo!	-	I'll smack you!
oritakatta	-	I wanted to get off

Common mistakes

mada tsuitenai	-	It's not on you anymore[14]

Day 19

shita ni itte ii yo	-	You can go downstairs
jibun de yatta deshou?	-	You did it by yourself, right? / It was your own fault, right?
Jiiji ni mou nai yo tte itte	-	Tell Grandpa there are no more
sou desu	-	That's right

Day 20

katazukete	-	Tidy up
futari to mo yatte kudasai	-	The two of you please do it
aeta	-	They were able to meet
mou ikkai yatte, tataite	-	Do it one more time, and hit it

---

[14] Should be '*mou tsuitenai*'.

Day 21

kore wa anata yo	-	This one is for you[15]
mimi ga nai	-	There are no crusts (on this bread)
kore wa muzukashii no	-	This is difficult
motto hayaku ga ii	-	Do it faster / Faster would be better

Day 22

nuttara iku yo	-	We will go when I've put it on (lipstick) [16]
Baaba to Jiiji inakunatchatta	-	Grandma and Grandpa have gone
Dumbo wa kaesu yo nee	-	We will return Dumbo (DVD), won't we?
okane motte kita no?	-	Did you bring some money?
sou da yo nee	-	That's right, isn't it[17]

Day 23

kitte kara bataa tsukeru	-	You put the butter on after cutting it
kiite kita yo	-	I went and asked her
karada ni warui yo	-	It's bad for your health
sukkiri shita	-	I feel refreshed / I feel much better
attameru?	-	Will you heat it up?[18]
gohan attametara tabereru	-	We can eat the rice when we have heated it up[19]

Day 24

sou ka na	-	Is that so, I wonder?
hantai yaru no	-	I'll do the other side
A-chan mite te	-	Watch A-chan

---

[15] Literally 'This is you'.
[16] '*nuru*' literally means 'to paint'.
[17] Previously A-chan used this phrase with a short '*ne*', which made it more of a question.
[18] '*attameru*' is a contraction of '*atatameru*' (to heat).
[19] '*tabereru*' is a contraction of '*taberareru*' (be able to eat).

ichigo no nioi shita yo	-	It smelled like strawberries[20]
Baaba to Jiiji okorarechau yo	-	Grandma and Grandpa will be angry with you[21]
aitara hairu	-	We'll go in when it opens
are? shizuka ni natchatta	-	Eh? It has gone quiet

Day 25

dare mo inakatta	-	Nobody was there
Okaasan nani moratta no?	-	What did Mummy get?
neru jikan da yo	-	It's time to go to sleep / It's bedtime
hayaku nenasai!	-	Go to sleep quickly! / Go to bed quickly!
anato warui yo	-	It's your fault / You are to blame
minna beruto shitenai yo	-	Nobody has done their seat-belt[22]

Day 26

mata kite kudasai ne	-	Please come again
dareka yaada! tte itta	-	Someone said "No!"
Okaasan, tora-san wa mitsukatta yo	-	Mummy, we found the tigers[23]
mata haitchatta	-	They went in again[24]

Day 27

se ga takai	-	He is tall[25]
atashi wa saki ne	-	I will go first, won't I?
kinou mo yatta yo nee	-	We did it yesterday too, didn't we

---

[20] The particle '*ga*' is implied: '*nioi ga shita*' (it smelled).
[21] '*okorarechau*' literally means 'You will have them be angry at you'. The particle '*ni*' is implied: '*Baaba to Jiiji ni okorarechau yo*'. Compare with '*Baaba to Jiiji ga okotchau*' (Grandma and Grandpa will be angry).
[22] Literally 'Everyone has not done their seat-belt'.
[23] '*mitsukatta*' (was found) is from '*mitsukaru*' (to be found), and '*mitsuketa*' (found) is from '*mitsukeru*' (to find). Both can mean 'I/we found it'.
[24] A-chan found stones in her shoes.
[25] The opposite of '*se ga takai*' (tall) is '*se ga hikui*' (short).

mite, shiro ni natta	-	Look, they have gone white

Day 28

Baaba to Jiiji ni miseyou nee	-	Let's show Grandma and Grandpa
Okaasan, chotto nemukunatchatta, A-chan	-	Mummy, A-chan has become a bit sleepy
konaida nokoshita deshou	-	You left some over the other day, right?
otetsudai shite kudasai	-	Please help me
mou sugu tsuku yo	-	We will arrive soon

Day 29

dare ga iru?	-	Who is there? / Who will be there?
Aladdin karite kita	-	We borrowed Aladdin / We rented Aladdin
A-chan zembu tabechatta	-	A-chan ate everything
utawanai de	-	Don't sing
mata omocha noreru yo	-	I'll be able to ride on the toys again
me tsuburanai deshou	-	We won't close our eyes, right?

Common mistakes

ugoite kudasai	-	Please move it[26]

Day 30

watashi no dakara	-	Because it's mine
aruite ikanai yo ne, watashitachi	-	We won't walk there, will we
yaranakute ii	-	We don't have to do it
mou ikkai hajimaru?	-	Will it start again?
Otousan to ikitai	-	I want to go with Daddy
shimattara ombu shite yaritai	-	When I've put them away, I want to have a piggy-back ride and do it

---

[26] Should be '*ugokashite kudasai*' (Please move it), since '*ugoite kudasai*' would mean 'Please move'.

Three years: Month five

Day 1

pantsu dashitenakatta deshou?	-	You haven't put my underpants out, right?
attakai kara kore kinakute ii	-	It's warm so I don't have to wear this
watashi kakureteru	-	I'm hiding
shinakute ii	-	You don't have to do it
omizu nonjatta kara omizu irete	-	I drank all the water so put some water in
A-chan ne, hitori de matteta no	-	A-chan was, you know, waiting by herself

Day 2

futatsu ni shiyou ka?	-	Shall we have two? / Shall we make it two?
koko ni suwaritai	-	I want to sit here
tataichau yo!	-	I'll smack you!
Shirayuki-hime boroboro doresu kiteru	-	Snow White is wearing a worn-out dress
kono kakkou	-	Looking like this[1]
D-san kiteru yo	-	D-san has come

Common mistakes

ookii yatsu mitsukatte	-	Find a big one[2]

Day 3

kobosanai de	-	Don't spill it
sandaru ni shite	-	Choose the sandals / Put the sandals on
kaze ga tomatta	-	The wind has stopped
hantai ni aru	-	It's on the other side
hidoi!	-	That's awful!
ikanakute ii no	-	You don't have to go

---

[1] Literally 'This appearance'.
[2] Should be '*ookii yatsu mitsukete*'.

Day 4

atashi datta no	-	It was me
A-chan koronjatte itakatta no, ashi	-	A-chan fell over and it hurt, my leg
watashi ga saki ni ikimasu kara	-	I will go first (so...)
boroboro doresu kinai yo	-	I won't wear the worn-out dress
onegai dakara kore ni shite	-	Please, I'm asking you, choose this one
hana tottara dame da ne	-	We mustn't pick the flowers

Day 5

dareka nusunjatta	-	Someone stole it
poketto mo atta	-	I found pockets too / It has pockets too
mada naottenai	-	It's not fixed yet
mite, suteki na ohana	-	Look, a lovely flower
ja, akiramemashou	-	Then, let's give up

Day 6

mitsukattara taberu	-	We will eat them when we find them
hora, suteki deshou?	-	See, isn't it lovely?
nande wakarimasen tte itta no?	-	Why did you say you don't understand?[3]
ato ikkai da yo	-	(Only) one more time
ato sankai tabetara owari da ne	-	We're finished when I eat three more times, aren't we
kore ga aiteru no	-	This is open

Day 7

dareka otoshichatta nee	-	Someone dropped it
mada nenne shiteru	-	She is still sleeping

---

[3] Literally 'Why did you say "I don't understand?"'. Compare with *'nande wakaranai tte itta no?'* which means 'Why did you say you don't understand?'. Both the quoted and unquoted forms are common in Japanese speech.

kaette kitara miyou nee	-	Let's watch it when we get home
te tsunaidenakatta	-	We weren't holding hands

Common mistakes

mou aru yo	-	There are still more[4]

Day 8

nani mo nai	-	There is nothing
kittenai deshou?	-	It's not cut, right?
kotchi ni shitara ii no	-	You should have this one
eigo shaberenai	-	I can't speak English[5]
makimodoshita n deshou?	-	You rewound it, right?[6]

Common mistakes

futatsu tora-san atta no	-	There were two tigers[7]

Day 9

himo yaranai de	-	Don't do the cord
kowasanai de, gurasu dakara	-	Don't break it, it's glass / It's glass so don't break it
ato sankai ne?	-	Three more times, isn't it?
namenai de	-	Don't lick it
nametara dame da yo	-	You mustn't lick it
sono ato wa...	-	After that...

Day 10

demo kietara kurakunaru	-	But if it goes out it will get dark
miruku to bisuketto taberareru	-	I can eat milk and biscuits
nanka nioi shita	-	Something smelled
chiisai no mo dekita	-	I did a small one too

---

[4] Should be '*mada aru yo*'.
[5] '*shaberenai*' is a contraction of '*shaberarenai*' (can't speak).
[6] '*makimodosu*' (to rewind) is often used for video tapes.
[7] Should be '*tora ga nihiki ita*'.

Common mistakes

sekkaku S-chan ni agechatta	-	S-chan gave it to me specially[8]

Day 11

koko ni ireta?	-	Did you put it in here?
D-san itsumo itteru nee	-	D-san is always going there isn't he
A-chan sankai yaru	-	A-chan will do it three times
soto de matteru?	-	Will you be waiting outside?
kono pan wa mazui yo!	-	This bread tastes really bad!
atashi tsukeru kara anata yatte	-	I'll put it on, so you do it

Day 12

atashi koko de matteru kara, dakara atchi de hamigaki shite	-	I'll be waiting here, so, you brush your teeth out there
osoto ga mieta	-	I can see outside[9]
sankai shita	-	I did it three times
nihongo de ii no	-	Japanese will do
A-chan hitori de A-chan no beddo de nenne shita no	-	A-chan slept by herself in A-chan's bed

Day 13

usagi-chan ninjin motteru	-	The rabbit has a carrot
warukunai	-	He's not bad / He's not evil
Okaasan ga tsukutta	-	Mummy made it
kudasai	-	Give it to me please
kore mo oishii	-	This is tasty too
motto hambaagu	-	More hamburger meat (please)

---

[8] Should be '*sekkaku S-chan ga kureta*'.
[9] Literally 'I could see outside' since '*mieta*' is past tense.

Day 14

asa denki tsukenai de	-	Don't turn the lights on in the morning
kutsu nuganai to	-	We have to take our shoes off
pan taberu ka?	-	Do you want to eat some bread?[10]
mou ikkai yaru ka?	-	Will we do it again? / Shall we do it again?

Notes

➤ A-chan is trying out the '-masu' form of all the verbs she knows.

Day 15

omokatta	-	It was heavy
Otousan itchatte, hitori de nenne shita no	-	Daddy went off, and I slept by myself
Okaasan ga osara koko ni oitchatte, dame da ne	-	Mummy put the plate here, and that's bad, isn't it
taihen deshou?	-	That's terrible, right? / That must be terrible
oshikko shimasu yo	-	I will do wees
dareka pinpon shita yo	-	Someone rang the doorbell
dekimashita?	-	Could you do it?[11]

Day 16

Otousan, jaketto iru yo, samui kara	-	Daddy, you'll need a jacket, because it's cold
shigoto mou owatta	-	I've already finished work
niteru dake	-	They just look alike
sakki itta deshou?	-	I told you before, right?[12]

---

[10] It is typically male speech to add '*ka?*' after the plain form of a verb like this.

[11] Here A-chan uses inflection to indicate a question, instead of the particle '*ka*'.

[12] '*itta*' here is from '*ui*' (to speak), not '*iku*' (to go).

oto ookii!	-	It's loud! / The noise is loud!

Day 17

A-chan, douro kuruma nai kara arukeru	-	There are no cars in the road, so A-chan can walk[13]
atashitachi ikanai yo ne	-	We won't go, will we[14]
tabeteru toki	-	When we are eating
tenki yohou hajimatta	-	The weather forecast has started
Okaasan to asonderu	-	I'm playing with Mummy
onaka ga suita	-	I'm hungry

Day 18

Otousan no tanjoubi owattara Baaba to Jiiji kuru yo	-	Grandma and Grandpa will come when Daddy's birthday is over
mada yatteru kara	-	I'm still doing it (so...)
suimingu no ato gohan tabenai to	-	We have to eat lunch after swimming
ii yo, shou ga nai	-	That's okay, it can't be helped

Day 19

mata ikitai naa	-	I'd like to go again
A-chan wa oiwai shinai	-	A-chan won't celebrate
Genie ga omizu ni haitte, dete kita	-	Genie went into the water, and came out
nani ga tsuiteru?	-	What's it got stuck on it?

Day 20

A-chan hikkaichatta	-	A-chan scratched
tsukatteru no ni!	-	Even though I'm using it...! / I'm using it![15]
hontou?	-	Really?

---

[13] The particle '*ni*' is implied: '... *douro ni*...'.
[14] '*atashitachi*' is a contraction of '*watashitachi*' (we).
[15] '*no ni*' means 'even though'. The remainder of the sentence is often left unsaid, in this case perhaps 'I'm using it... and you took it away'.

daisuki datta	-	I loved it
Otousan motte itte	-	Daddy, take it with you
oshikko shita yo, gohan no mae ni	-	I did wees, before dinner[16]

Day 21

A-chan no daiji na hime-sama da yo	-	It's A-chan's precious princess
kiiro no baggu ni haitteta	-	It was in the yellow bag
amakute oishii tabemono datta nee	-	It was sweet and tasty food, wasn't it
atarashii ouchi ja nai	-	It's not a new house
ii yo, arau to ochiru yo	-	It's okay, it will come out in the wash[17]
mada futteru	-	It's still raining

Day 22

kiiro no me na no	-	They are yellow eyes
kaechau yo	-	I'll change it
chotto koko ni ochichatta	-	A bit fell down here / Some fell down here
dou shiyou ka naa?	-	I wonder what shall we do?
suwatte, kou yatte, asobitai no	-	I want to sit, do this, and play
ochichattara taihen da yo	-	It will be terrible if you fall off

Day 23

nihongo ni shita yo, D-san ga	-	D-san set it (the DVD) into Japanese
Okaasan akachan to tomaru	-	Mummy will stay with the baby
datte, minai yo nee	-	Well, because we won't see it
atode kuru no?	-	Will they come later?
ja, kyou akachan ni kaou ka?	-	Then, shall we buy it for the baby today?

---

[16] '*mae*' means 'before'.
[17] '*to*' here is short for '*toki*' (when), so this literally means 'It's okay, it will come out when you wash it'.

datte, anata ga shita n deshou?	-	Well, because you did it, right?

Common mistakes

chigau ni shite	-	Choose a different one[18]

Day 24

tsumetai no tsukattara ii no ni	-	I wish you would use the cold one[19]
akachan to kenka shitara dame	-	You mustn't fight with the baby
mou ikkai yatte miyou	-	Let's try it one more time
konsento tsukete ne	-	Turn it on at the wall socket
akai iro no hou ni itte kudasai	-	Please go in the red-coloured direction

Common mistakes

okiru no jikan	-	Time to get up[20]

Day 25

happa ga ochite kichatta	-	The leaves have fallen down
hen da	-	It's strange
doresu ga hen da	-	The dress is strange / The dress looks funny
mou hayaku isoide!	-	Quick, hurry up!

Day 26

fundeta	-	I was treading on it
Minnie-chan ja nakute...	-	Not Minnie Mouse...
sono geemu yatta no	-	We played that game
muzukashii yo nee	-	It's difficult, isn't it

---

[18] Should be '*chigau no ni shite*'.
[19] '*-tara ii no ni*' literally means 'even though it would be good if...'.
[20] Should be '*okiru jikan*'.

Day 27

mou ookikunatchatta	-	It's bigger now / It's already bigger
minakute ii	-	You don't have to watch it
matte kureru?	-	Would you wait for me?
nande tsuiteru?	-	Why is it turned on?
waratteru n ja nai	-	It's not something to laugh at / I'm not laughing at it

Day 28

omutsu ja nakute Minnie-chan no pantsu dakara botan shinakute ii	-	It's not a nappy, it's Minnie Mouse's underpants, so we don't have to do the buttons
tabete kureru?	-	Would you eat it for me?
ja, oroshite	-	Then, put it down
kikanakute ii	-	We don't have to listen to it
Otousan shawaa shite, mukou no hou de	-	Daddy, have a shower, over there
kinou ame ga futta	-	It rained yesterday

Day 29

ii desu	-	No thank you
mou sugu naoru yo	-	You will get well soon
demo mada naoranai	-	But you won't get well yet
mae ni tsuiteru	-	It's stuck on the front
mite mite, atchi kara deta	-	Look, look, it came out from there
akachan umareta kara neko-chan sawatte mo ii nee	-	The baby has been born so I can touch cats now, can't I

Day 30

zembu tabetara onaka itakunatchau yo	-	If you eat them all your stomach will hurt[21]
tatte kureru?	-	Would you stand up for me?
mite koyou	-	Let's go and see

---

[21] '*itakunatchau*' literally means 'will become painful'.

kyou no gohan wa nan desu ka?	-	What is today's dinner?

Common mistakes

ochiteru no toki, yubi itakatta	-	My finger hurt when I fell[22]

---

[22] Should be '*ochita toki, yubi itakatta*'.

Three years: Month six

Day 1

onaka sukanai yo	-	I won't get hungry
waa, tanoshii!	-	Oh, this is fun!
shimpai shinai de	-	Don't worry
ohi-sama ga deta kara attakai	-	It's warm because the sun has come out[1]
yasashikute kawaii	-	She is kind and cute

Common mistakes

tebukuro no tsukeru no toki, A-chan ga ichimai no te ga tsumetakunatchau	-	While A-chan puts on her gloves, one hand gets cold[2]

Day 2

A-chan ga nakushichatta	-	A-chan lost it
nande kowareteru no?	-	Why is it broken?
demo kore wa aru	-	But we have this
kurukuru shiteru	-	It's curly
kite kureru?	-	Would you come with me?
chuu shite kureru?	-	Would you kiss me?

Day 3

datte, mada aru n da mon	-	Well, because there are still some left[3]
chanto mottara ii	-	You should hold it properly
hen na kao shiteru	-	He's making a funny face
mae wa yogoreteru	-	The front is dirty
kou wa ii yo, kou wa dame	-	This way is good, this way is bad

---

[1] '*ohi-sama*' is a children's word for '*hi*' (sun).
[2] Should be '*tebukuro o tsuketeru aida ni A-chan no katate ga tsumetakunatchau*'.
[3] '*da mon*' is a contraction of '*da mono*'. It is often used with '*datte*' to give an indignant explanation. For example, '*datte, hontou nan da mon!*' (Well, because it's true!).

sugoi tanoshikatta	-	It was really fun

Day 4

iro ga kawatteru yo	-	The colours are changing
hitsuji kami tabeteta	-	The sheep was eating my hair
shita ni denki tsuiteru mitai	-	The lights seem to be on downstairs
datte, kowakunatchau	-	Well, because I'll get scared
mou ikkai yaranai to	-	We have to do this once more
onaka suiteru mitai	-	She seems to be hungry
ii no ga aru yo	-	I have a good one

Day 5

seki ga mada naottenai kara ikanakunatchau	-	My cough is not better yet so I won't be able to go[4]
motto aru	-	There are more
A-chan umaretenakatta	-	A-chan wasn't born
demo dou yatte taberu deshou?	-	But how would you eat it?
me ga akai	-	Your eyes are red

Common mistakes

sanko buta-san ga ita	-	There were three pigs[5]

Day 6

Okaasan ni neko-chan ga ouchi ni kuru yo nee tte itte miyou	-	Let's tell Mummy a cat is going to come to our house
miruku ageteru	-	She is giving her milk
shichiji ni nattara akachan irete ne	-	Put the baby in when it is 7 o'clock
ja, Otousan to katazukeyou	-	Then, let's clear up with Daddy
zembu da yo!	-	All of them!

---

[4] *'ikanakunatchau'* literally means 'become that I will not go'. Compare this to *'ikenakunatchau'* (become unable to go).
[5] Should be *'buta ga sambiki ita'*.

Common mistakes

akachan no hou ni te tsunaida	-	I went over to the baby and held her hand[6]

Day 7

nan to kaita no?	-	What did you write? / What's written there?
tanoshikatta naa	-	It was so much fun
Okaasan, akachan motanai no?	-	Mummy, won't the baby hold it?
soshite yajirushi oshite	-	And then press the arrow
kande tabete	-	Chew your food[7]
motto yaritakatta no ni!	-	I wanted to do more!

Day 8

koko ni haittara ii no ni	-	I wish you would go in here
dasanai de, aru kara ne	-	Don't get them out, I (already) have some
koko ni konakatta	-	They didn't come here
burokku ni butsukatchatta	-	I bumped into the blocks

Common mistakes

atsukattenai	-	It wasn't hot[8]

Day 9

kono yooguruto daisuki	-	I love this yogurt
yooguruto taberu kara Otousan kudasai	-	I'll eat the yogurt so Daddy please give me some
A-chan no beddo ni isshoni itakatta	-	I wanted to be together in A-chan's bed
kawaitara kireru	-	I can wear it when it dries

---

[6] Should be '*akachan no hou ni itte, te tsunaida*'.
[7] Literally 'Chew it and eat it'.
[8] In reply to '*atsukatta?*' (Was it hot?). Should be '*atsukunakatta*' (It wasn't hot).

demo yoru wa konakatta	- But they didn't come in the evening
ashita katte kite	- Go and buy some tomorrow
pan dake taberu	- I will just eat bread

Day 10

atatakakatta	- It was warm
taihen da ne	- That's terrible, isn't it
Okaasan ga kigaeru yo	- Mummy will change clothes
gambatta nee, Okaasan	- You tried really hard, didn't you Mummy
otomodachi ni akachan umareta yo tte itte	- Tell my friends the baby was born

Day 11

asa wa denki tsukenai!	- We don't turn lights on in the morning!
mou futtenai	- It's not raining anymore
miruku kudasai tte itteru no	- I'm saying please give me some milk
mou katazuketa yo	- I already tidied up
zutto A-chan no beddo de nenne shite, asa ni natta	- I slept the whole time in A-chan's bed, and then it was morning
neko-chan miruku nameteru no	- The cat is licking the milk

Day 12

gakkou ga mieru	- I can see school
minna kiteru jan	- Everyone is wearing them
A-chan dakko shitai	- A-chan wants to hold her (the baby)
kami ga nagakunatchatta	- My hair has become longer
kiranai to	- I'll have to cut it

Day 13

oshikko shite kuru	- I'll go and do wees
Otousan, ouma-san ni noritai nee	- Daddy, you want to ride a horse, don't you
owattara omocha sawatte ii no	- You can touch the toys when you have finished

aketara toire ni ikou ne	-	Let's go to the toilet after we open them
subetchatta	-	I slipped

Day 14

mabushii yo	-	It's too bright / It's glaring
mieru yo, Okaasan ga	-	I can see you, Mummy
atchitchi!	-	Ouch, it's hot!
motto kureru?	-	Can I have some more?

Common mistakes

A-chan wa akachan ni natteru toki	-	When A-chan was a baby[9]

Day 15

unchi shiteru mitai	-	She seems to be doing poos
A-chan nemuttai!	-	A-chan is sleepy![10]
A-chan akachan no toki chiisakatta	-	A-chan was small when she was a baby
yon-sai ni nattara keeki moraeru	-	I can have a cake when I turn four

Common mistakes

A-chan to utau no toki wa ii ko ni shiteru yo	-	She is a good girl when she sings with A-chan[11]

Day 16

A-chan motte kuru kara nani ga ii?	-	A-chan will bring it so what do you want?
mada kowareteru	-	It's still broken
A-chan to nakayoku shiteru	-	A-chan is getting along well with her
te aratte kiyou ka?	-	Shall we wash hands and put it on (clothes)?

---

[9] Should be '*A-chan wa akachan no toki*'.
[10] '*nemuttai*' is a casual form of '*nemutai*' (sleepy), used to add emphasis.
[11] '*utau no toki*' should be '*utau toki*' (when she sings).

kaado moraenakunatchau yo	-	You won't be able to get a card
mae ni itte	-	You say it first

Day 17

pan to isshoni tabenai to	-	We have to eat it with bread
mou ii desu ka?	-	May I start? / Are we ready now?
ma ni atta!	-	We made it in time!
tatanderu	-	I'm folding them up

Day 18

supuun kureru?	-	Can I have a spoon?
koori-makura motte kuru	-	I'll go and get the ice-pillow / I'll bring the ice-pillow
netsu hakatta no	-	I took my temperature
zutto iru	-	I will be here the whole time

Common mistakes

dore no masuku?	-	Which mask?[12]

Day 19

ippai de ii no?	-	Is a lot okay? / Is it okay to fill it up?
Okaasan ni A-chan kusuri nonda yo tte itte ne	-	Tell Mummy that A-chan drank the medicine, won't you?
D-chan hanakande gomi suteta	-	D-chan blew her nose and threw the rubbish away[13]
kega shichau	-	You will get hurt

Common mistakes

mado ni itakatta	-	I hurt myself on the window[14]

---

[12] Should be '*dono masuku?*'.
[13] '*hanakande*' is from '*hanakamu*', which is a contraction of '*hana o kamu*' (to blow one's nose).
[14] Should be '*mado de itakatta*'.

Day 20

zettai A-chan okotchau no	-	A-chan will definitely get angry
A-chan gambatta kara gohan tabetara kore taberu	-	A-chan tried really hard, so she will eat this after having dinner
Otousan saki ni tabenai de	-	Daddy don't eat before us
N-chan to A-chan zutto Oosutoraria ni iru	-	N-chan and A-chan will be in Australia the whole time
A-chan onaka suichatta kara motto oyatsu kureru?	-	A-chan is hungry so can she have more snacks?
nihongo wa katatsumuri, eigo wa wakaranai	-	The Japanese is 'snail', I don't know the English

Day 21

kore zenzen aji shinai yo nee	-	This doesn't taste of anything at all, does it
A-chan ue ni itte N-chan mita yo	-	A-chan went upstairs and saw N-chan
N-chan daaisuki!	-	I love N-chan![15]
A-chan itta no oboeteru	-	A-chan remembers going[16]
D-chan wa yasumi datta	-	D-chan was away

Common mistakes

N-chan motte iku?	-	Will we take N-chan?[17]

Day 22

sou yatte oboeteru	-	That's how I remember it
A-chan ga ireru	-	A-chan will put it in
ashita sore taberu yo ne	-	We will eat that tomorrow, won't we
Okaasan, soko ni oite mo ii desu ka?	-	Mummy, may I leave it there?

---

[15] '*daisuki*' (love) can be stretched to '*daaisuki*' for emphasis.
[16] The particle '*o*' is implied: '*A-chan itta no o oboeteru*'.
[17] Should be '*N-chan tsurete iku?*', since '*motte iku*' (take) is only for inanimate objects.

kuruma kichau kara A-chan butsukatchau kara sore wa taihen	-	Cars will come, so A-chan will get hit, so that would be terrible[18]

Day 23

A-chan me tsubutteru yo	-	A-chan has her eyes closed
doa shimatchau yo, warui kedo	-	The doors are closing, please excuse me[19]
sore wa itasou	-	That sounds painful / That looks painful
muri shite tabenai de, Okaasan	-	Don't force yourself to eat, Mummy[20]
Otousan ni itteru no	-	I'm talking to Daddy

Day 24

Okaasan, Otousan ga A-chan gorira tte itteru	-	Mummy, Daddy says A-chan is a gorilla
Okaasan, Otousan oyatsu nai tte itteru	-	Mummy, Daddy says there are no snacks
ryoute de yaranai to	-	You have to do it with both hands
barabara ni shitara ii yo	-	You should take it apart
N-chan iru kara ikenakunatchau	-	You can't go because N-chan is here

Day 25

hambunko da yo	-	It's half each / There's half for each of us
Otousan, N-chan no atama ookikunatchatta	-	Daddy, N-chan's head got bigger
gomi ni sutechatta	-	I threw it in the rubbish
karakatta kara omizu nonderu	-	It was spicy so I'm drinking water
kyou ame futtenai kara kuruma de ikanakute mo ii desu	-	It's not raining today so we don't have to go by car

---

[18] The Japanese here is just as awkward as the English.
[19] '*warui kedo*' literally means 'It is bad of me, but...'.
[20] '*muri suru*' means 'to overdo it' or 'to force'.

Day 26

itadakimasu! shinai to	-	We have to go "Let's eat!"
muri shite tabenakute ii	-	You don't have to force yourself to eat it
muri shite tabenai	-	I won't force myself to eat it
soko ni oitara ii n da	-	You should put it there / You can put it there
aruite ikanai to	-	We have to walk there
shita ni ochiteta	-	It had fallen down / It was on the floor

Day 27

eigo dake aru no	-	There is only English
oishikute amai	-	It's tasty and sweet
A-chan seki ga deru kara kuruma de iku	-	We will go by car because A-chan has a cough
kinou sugoku naiteta	-	Yesterday she cried terribly
kukkii ga yakete imasu	-	The cookies are baking

Day 28

Okaasan mizugi ni natchau?	-	Mummy will you be in your swimsuit?
yubi ga hasamatchau	-	Your fingers will get caught
sore wa tanoshisou	-	That sounds like fun / That looks like fun
Otousan, gohan no toki wa pasokon yaranai!	-	Daddy, we don't do computer at meal time!
watashi ga naoseru yo	-	I can fix it
soshite?	-	And then?

Day 29

oshikko ikitakunakunatchatta	-	I don't need to go and do wees now[21]
hikkakatchatta, doa ni	-	It got caught, in the door

---

[21] '*ikitakunakunatchatta*' literally means 'become not wanting to go'.

Three years: Month six

kigaenai to	-	You have to get changed
ii n ja nai?	-	Isn't that okay?[22]
oshikko fuku ne	-	I will wipe up the wees
fukanakatta	-	I didn't wipe it up

Day 30

Okaasan, Otousan ga tsukaisugita	-	Mummy, Daddy used too much
Otousan kigaetenakatta	-	Daddy hadn't changed clothes
sore nani?	-	What's that?
yurashite kudasai	-	Please rock it / Please swing it
ashi ga samusou dakara hiitaa tsukenai to	-	Your legs look cold so you must turn the heater on
watashi ga dasu ne	-	I will get them out
nande koboshiteru no?!	-	Why are you spilling it?!
watashi mo sugoku tanoshii	-	I am really happy too

Day 31

sugoku nagai	-	It's really long
Okaasan, taitsu doko ni aru no?	-	Mummy, where are my tights?
sugoku tanoshii no	-	It's so much fun
daikon sugoku taberu yo	-	I eat loads of radish
asonderu baai ja nai!	-	This is no time for playing!
N-chan mainichi ofuro ni hairu nee	-	N-chan has a bath every day

---

[22] Previously '*ii ja nai?*'.

Final Comments

The order in which A-chan has learned Japanese grammar is remarkably different to the order it is normally taught in Japanese courses and textbooks. In addition to using the casual level of speech, some of the key differences are:

- ➤ A-chan uses the particle *'ga'* by default instead of the particle *'wa'*. She only uses *'wa'* to put particular emphasis on a word to distinguish it from other possibilities. As previously noted, the use of *'wa'* as often taught in textbooks can sound childish. It also tends to make students start every sentence unnaturally with a noun or personal pronoun followed by *'wa'*, for example *'watashi wa...'* (I...).

- ➤ Textbooks teach that *'ee'* means 'yes' and *'iie'* means 'no'. However, to mean 'yes' A-chan says *'hai'* or uses expressions like *'sou sou'*. For 'no' she usually says *'chigau'* or replies using a negative verb. For example *'ikanai'* (No, I won't go) or *'iranai'* (No, I don't want it).

- ➤ A-chan learned vocabulary as the words became relevant to her situation: She learned *'hanasu'* with the meaning of 'to let go' before meaning 'to speak'. She learned *'yomu'* with the meaning of 'to call' before meaning 'to read'. She tends to use 'iru' to mean 'want' rather than 'need'.

- ➤ A-chan uses *'deshou'* to mean 'right?' or 'right!', for example *'abunai deshou!'* (It's dangerous, right!). Textbooks first teach *'deshou'* to mean 'probably'.

- ➤ Most of A-chan's speech patterns are shorter than their more technically correct equivalents: She says *'dotchi ga ii?'* (Which do you want?') rather than *'dotchi no hou ga ii?'*. She uses conversational contractions like *'attakai'* for 'atatakai' (warm), and 'tabereru' for 'taberareru' (can eat). She uses the '-te' verb form followed by 'tte itta', instead of the '-ru' verb form with 'you ni itta'. For example, she would say 'tabete tte itta', rather than 'taberu you ni itta' to mean 'She said to eat it'.

Putting it together

Here is the entire transcript of a short one-way 'conversation' A-chan had on the telephone when she was exactly 3 years old:

> "moshi moshi. Otousan osoi desu ne. hayaku kaette kite. kaettara asobou yo. mada tabete nai deshou? dakara onaka suiteru. ja, hayaku kaette ne. baibai."

> "Hello. You're late Daddy! Hurry up and come home. Let's play when you get home. You haven't eaten yet, right? That's why you're always hungry. Well, hurry home okay? Bye bye."

You can see here the lack of particles such as 'wa' and 'ga' between words. She uses a mixture of set phrases such as 'hayaku kaette kite' (hurry home) together with the simple grammar needed to convey her meaning.

A-chan generally seems to plan each phrase before she begins to speak it, but only up to the next comma or period. She tends to use short phrases, and speaks rapidly, often barely pausing between sentences.

Although the conversation above is simple, it is correct and sounds natural. Most importantly, A-chan has succeeded in making herself understood, and that is what learning a language is all about.

Verb Reference

ageru	give	*hakaru*	measure
akeru	open	*haku*	wear below the waist
akirameru	give up; abandon	*hanareru*	be apart
aku	open	*hanasu*	let go
arau	wash	*haru*	stick; paste; affix
aru	be (inanimate objects); have	*hasamaru*	be caught in
aruku	walk	*hasamu*	sandwich; hold between
asobu	play; enjoy oneself	*hashiru*	run
atatameru	warm; heat	*hikkaku*	scratch
au	match	*hipparu*	pull
au	meet	*hiraku*	open
butsukaru	bump into	*hirou*	pick up; find
chigau	be different	*iku*	go
dasu	get out; put out	*ireru*	put in; insert
dekakeru	go out; leave the house	*iru*	be (animate objects)
dekiru	be able to do; be ready	*iru*	need; want
deru	go out; leave; appear	*isogu*	hurry
dokasu	move (something); get (something) out of the way	*itadaku*	receive
		iu	say; call
doku	move out of the way	*kaburu*	wear on head
		kaeru	change
erabu	choose	*kaeru*	return
fuku	wipe	*kaesu*	return (something); put back; send back
fumu	tread on		
furu	fall	*kakeru*	put on; sprinkle; pour
gambaru	try one's best	*kaku*	write; draw
hairu	enter	*kaku*	sweat
hajimaru	begin	*kakureru*	hide
		kamu	bite; chew

kangaeru	think about	*mawasu*	turn (something)
kariru	rent; borrow	*mieru*	be able to see
kasu	lend	*miru*	see
katazukeru	tidy up; put away	*miseru*	show
kau	buy	*mitsukaru*	find
kawaku	dry	*mitsukeru*	find (something)
kawaru	change	*modosu*	put back
kazoeru	count	*morau*	receive
kesu	turn off	*moreru*	leak
kieru	go out; go off	*motsu*	have; hold
kigaeru	change clothes	*nagasu*	flush
kikoeru	be able to hear	*nageru*	throw
kiku	listen	*naku*	cry
kimeru	decide	*nakusu*	lose
kireru	break off	*nameru*	lick
kiru	wear above the waist	*naoru*	get well; be fixed
kiru	cut	*naosu*	fix
koboreru	spill	*naru*	become
kobosu	spill (something)	*neru*	sleep
komu	be crowded	*niru*	look alike
korobu	fall down; fall over	*nobasu*	extend; stretch
kowareru	break	*nokosu*	leave behind; leave over
kowasu	break (something)	*nomu*	drink
kureru	receive	*nugu*	take off clothes
kuru	come	*nureru*	get wet
kuttsuku	stick to	*nuru*	paint
machigaeru	make a mistake	*nusumu*	steal
machigau	be wrong	*oboeru*	remember
makimodosu	rewind	*ochiru*	fall
matsu	wait	*ochitsuku*	calm down
mawaru	turn	*odoru*	dance
		okiru	wake up; get up

Verb Reference 187

okoru	be angry	*tojiru*	close
oku	put; place; leave	*tomaru*	stop; halt
omou	think	*tomaru*	stay
oriru	get off; get down	*tomeru*	stop (something)
orosu	take down; put down	*toreru*	be able to reach
		toru	take; take a photo
oshieru	teach; tell	*tsuburu*	close (eyes)
osu	push	*tsukamaeru*	catch
otosu	drop	*tsukamaru*	hold on; be arrested
owaru	finish; end		
oyogu	swim	*tsukamu*	hold on
sagasu	search	*tsukareru*	get tired
saku	bloom	*tsukau*	use
sasu	sting; pierce	*tsukeru*	attach; turn on
sawaru	touch	*tsuku*	be attached
shaberu	talk	*tsuku*	arrive
shimau	finish; close	*tsukuru*	make
shimeru	close (something)	*tsunagu*	connect
shiru	know	*ugoku*	move
suberu	slip; slide	*ugokasu*	move (something)
suku	become empty	*umareru*	be born
suru	do	*utau*	sing
suteru	throw away	*wakaru*	understand; know
suwaru	sit	*warau*	laugh
taberu	eat	*wasureru*	forget
tasukeru	help; save; rescue	*yaku*	cook; bake; toast; grill; burn
tataku	knock; strike; smack	*yameru*	stop; cease
tatamu	fold	*yamu*	end; be over
tatsu	stand	*yaru*	do
tetsudau	help	*yogoreru*	get dirty
tobu	fly; jump	*yomu*	read
todoku	reach; be delivered	*yurasu*	rock; swing

Made in the USA
Lexington, KY
18 November 2013